How to Succeed with an Education

by: George Lisenko

Table of Contents

Dedication	14
Acknowledgements	15
About the Author	16
Nina, Galina, and Freida Meet Albert and George	17
Early Life: Emigrants and Netherlands	23
Coming to America	25
Growing Up: Melting Into the Pot	27
Crime Times	31
Time to Be a Soldier	40
Vietnam Era	45
I'm Coming Home	76
Back to Civilian Life (Marriage to Lelah)	77
Raising Kids	79
Back to Single Life (Divorce from Lelah)	91
Disco Fever	93
Ana Fever	97
Career Advancement	100
The Father of All Calls	103
…and the Horse You Rode in Place on	112
Niki and the Last of the USSR	115
Karen and trip to vegas	122
Around the World In 80 Months	128
The United States of America v George Lisenko	140
Potent Omni and the Rising Bottom Line	146
The Leftists Ain't Right and MAGA Trumps Them All	151
Looking Back	155
In Closing	156
Hobbies and Collections	157
Family and Friends	178
Favorite Movies	233
Stories from Others	235
From Frieda	235
From Jim and Alexis	236
From Denise	240
From Olga	255
From Victor	256
From Karen	266

From Lynne...268

From Ana...269

From Lenny..271

From Alexandra 273

From Niki...275

In closing notes: 277

Table of Figures

Figure 1 Year 1945 - Albert Abda letters to his parents (1 of 2) 20

Figure 2 Year 1945 - Albert Abda letter to his parents (2 of 2)....................................21

Figure 3 Family tree descending from John and Diamond Abda 22

Figure 4 Year 1954 - Queen Wilhelmina –The Netherlands - She handed out blue handkerchiefs to all the kids and my sister and I still have ours. 23

Figure 5 Olga, Mom, Victor, and Yura (Victor II). Once my sister and I were gone, they were one happy family. 24

Figure 6 Year 1957 – Campbell Ave. and Cortez St. – Chicago, IL – The first place we lived coming from Germany - 2nd floor left where there a Bears banner is. 25

Figure 7 Year 1957 - Frederic Chopin Elementary School – Chicago, IL...................26

Figure 8 Year 1957 – Paul Anka...27

Figure 9 Year 1958 – The Monotones 27

Figure 10 Year 1958 – Danny and the Juniors...27

Figure 11 Year 1960 – Neil Sedaka 27

Figure 12 Year 1960 – Elvis Presley 27

Figure 13 Year 1960 – Steve Lawrence...27

Figure 14 Year 1961 – Roy Orbison 28

Figure 15 Year 1961 - Jarmels 28

Figure 16 Year 1962 – The Contours...28

Figure 17 Year 1963 – The Ronettes 28

Figure 18 Year 1964 – Roy Orbison 28

Figure 19 Year 1965 – The Righteous Brothers 28

Figure 20 Year 1960 – Marty Robbins 29

Figure 21 Year 1959 - Dion 29

Figure 22 Year 1960 – Marty Robbins 29

Figure 23 Year 1964 – Four Tops..29

Figure 24 Year 1962 – The 4 Seasons 29

Figure 25 Year 1965 – The Vogues 29

Figure 26 Year 1961 – Gene Pitney 29

Figure 27 Year 1961 – The Tokens 29

Figure 28 Year 1963 – Chicago and Western Gang (my gang) 31

Figure 29 The types of crosses I made 32

Figure 30 Year 1963 - John F. Kennedy, the 35th President of the United States, sitting with his wife, Jacqueline Kennedy. He was shot in the head while riding in a motorcade in Dallas, Texas, on November 22, 1963 33

Figure 31 Year 1963 – George Lisenko 35

Figure 32 Year 1953 – Chevy Bel-Air 36

Figure 33 Year 1963 – Gas Prices 36

Figure 34 Year 1964 – My time 38

Figure 35 Year 1965 – I started boot camp in San Diego, CA, in January of 1965. My life was completely turned around, that's for sure, as it became a series of "Yes, sirs" and "No, sirs". 40

Figure 36 George Lisenko sitting down with gun 41

Figure 37 Year 1966 - Guard Roster 41

Figure 38 Just out of Boot Camp with my Marine friends visiting Tijuana, Mexico in 1965 – Me, George Lange, Danny Rudd, and several other friends 42

Figure 39 Six of my friends from my squad 43

Figure 40 Camp Hansen, Okinawa 43

Figure 41 Aiming a grenade launcher 43

Figure 42 Last days in Naha, Okinawa, before shipping to Vietnam. Me (bottom left picture) and my good friend, John, who I called E.J. (bottom right picture) 44

Figure 43 Badges for George's USMC teams 45

Figure 44 Life on ship. Tight quarters, muster drills, all of your possessions in a duffel bag, and sleeping racks stacked five high. 45

Figure 45 Helo transport picking up troops in a rice paddy 46

Figure 46 Giant snakes, rats, centipedes, mosquitoes. It seemed like this was an every-day-type thing.... 46

Figure 47 Troop life in Viet Nam involved a lot of marching and vigilance. Vietnamese currency and political cartoons (right). 47

Figure 48 U.S. tank moving across a field. Air strike visible on the horizon. 48

Figure 49 Some of the traps the Viet Cong laid for us. 48

Figure 50 It was a big deal to have a body count for the Top Brass 49

Figure 51 Another body count for the Top Brass. It was very sad, but this is the way it was. This is what I saw when I first arrived..50

Figure 52 Viet Cong prisoners of war...50

Figure 53 Viet Cong spiked booby trap 51

Figure 54 Explosions and fires as the war was fought near Vietnamese villages.................................51

Figure 55 Various bathing situations during the war 52

Figure 56 U.S. troops landing at a Vietnamese beach 52

Figure 57 Eating VFC (Vietnam Fried Chicken)..53

Figure 58 Artillery 53

Figure 59 Medics tending to a wounded soldier 53

Figure 60 Helicopter troop transports, artillery, and support aircraft 54

Figure 61 Armor units arriving via boat 54

Figure 62 Burning Viet Cong encampments. Viet Cong pungee pit trap and two examples of swinging spiked traps. 55

Figure 63 Laying low during a nearby airstrike, flying in a helicopter, interacting with local children.....56

Figure 64 It seemed like we were on the choppers at least 2 - 3 times a week, going in and out of the rice paddies or jungles. This was my life..57

Figure 65 Various munitions - rifle rounds and explosives 57

Figure 66 Helicopter sortie, M60 7.62 caliber machine gun...58

Figure 67 M60 7.62 caliber machine gun and shoulder-fired Rocket-Propelled Grenade (RPG) 58

Figure 68 .50 caliber machine gun nest, mortar, and local wildlife..58

Figure 69 In 1966, my buddy with an M1966-60 machine gun, doing his thing! 59

Figure 70 Vietnamese girl with a dropped U.S. Bomb that did not go off...59

Figure 71 Year 1966 – Operation Utah and Chu Lai - As you can see in the picture, two bullets hit my gun belt. One went through my canteen, and the other grazed my magazine, just missing the primer. 60

Figure 72 Napalm airstrike. It seemed like this was an everyday type thing! 61

Figure 73 Some of the weapons we captured..62

Figure 74 Riding on a tank in a sandbag nest 62

Figure 75 Some of the kids from the local villages 63

Figure 76 It seems that the village kids were always after me because I always gave them candy bars and whatever I could...63

Figure 77 Year 1966 – Da Nang, Vietnam 64

Figure 78 Vietnamese currency 65

Figure 79 I didn't see the pictures I sent home until years later. I took over 300 pictures; the more I was told not to take pictures, the more I took, to let the pictures do the talking for me. 66

Figure 80 George Lisenko's Combat History 66

Figure 81 George Lisenko, USMC. 67

Figure 82 Villagers using elephants 67

Figure 83 George Lisenko, his bullet-proof canteen, and a Vietnamese villager. 68

Figure 84 Newspaper clippings about the Vietnam War. 69

Figure 85 Troop transports, investigating a Viet Cong tunnel, local villagers, and a rice paddy. 70

Figure 86 Marching 71

Figure 87 Riding on Armored Personnel Carriers (APCs) 71

Figure 88 Group prayer while deployed 72

Figure 89 Vietnamese currency, church service on deployment, and Chinook helicopters 72

Figure 90 Medical helicopter transport, Vietnamese town, a destroyed home, and a rat found in the bivouac 73

Figure 91 U.S. infantry transportation and Vietnamese transportation. 73

Figure 92 U.S. troops awaiting the arrival of helicopters 74

Figure 93 This is a monument in Washington, D.C. – A must-see! 75

Figure 94 Year 1967 – George Lisenko & Lelah Ann Fisher (wedding pictures) 77

Figure 95 Year 1964 - Pontiac Bonneville 78

Figure 96 Year 1968 – Top left: Lelah 3 months pregnant. Top right: Lelah carrying Lynne. Bottom left: Lynn Marie (my daughter). Bottom right: Lynne with my mom. 79

Figure 97 George, Lelah, and Lynn 80

Figure 98 Year 1969 – Plymouth GTX 440 80

Figure 99 Dodge Charger big block 440 81

Figure 100 Figure 81 Dodge Challenger after Lelah drove it off a cliff. 82

Figure 101 Picture of Mickey and his wife, Debbie, as well as Danny and his wife. Both of them had dune buggies. 83

Figure 102 Records from 1966 – 1969 84

Figure 103 Year 1969 – Woodstock and hippies 85

Figure 104 Records from the early 1970s. 85

Figure 105 My beautiful mother, Galina. I miss her more and more with each day that goes by. I can't help but tear up when I look at her pictures. To me, she was the best mother one could ask for. She was very talented and could do almost anything. 86

Figure 106 George and his accidental owl 87

Figure 107 My Dune Boggy days with the Over the Hill Gang (picture taken in early '70s in Glamis Sand Dunes 88

Figure 108 My Mom, Step Dad at Olgas Wedding Day 89

Figure 109 "We Just Disagree" by Dave Mason - This song reminded me of my Lelah 91

Figure 110 Records from the late 1970s. 92

Figure 111 George's photoshoots 93

Figure 112 George Lisenko during his disco days (c. 1981) 94

Figure 113 My Disco days. I loved to dance; I won some money and some other stuff for first place in dance competitions. Those days were a lot of fun. 95

Figure 114 1977 Pontiac, Trans AM 96

Figure 115 My beautiful wife, Ana. What more could a man ask for? She is beautiful, a great dancer, my best friend, and my lover! I have to say: this was the best time of my life. 98

Figure 116 George and Ana's wedding in Las Vegas on May 12, 1984, ... 99

Figure 117 Lenny's rooftop artwork and some of the machines at Omni 101

Figure 118 Year 2005 (approx.) - Some of Lenny's artistry on the 12,000 square foot Omni building, photographed by a helicopter flying above the building. 102

Figure 119 Year 1985 - Letter from Albert Abda (1 of 2) 104

Figure 120 Year 1985 - Letter from Albert Abda (2 of 2) 105

Figure 121 George, Ana, and Alexandra Marie 106

Figure 122 Year 1990 - Alex at 5 years old 107

Figure 123 Year 1986 - Obituary for Albert Abda 107

Figure 124 Year 1986 (late December) – I love this picture with my two beautiful sisters. Left: Denise? Middle: Me. Right: Alexis 109

Figure 125 George, Niki, Irma, Ana, and Alexis 109

Figure 126 Irma 110

Figure 127 Alexis, Irma, and Niki celebrating Irma's 101st birthday 110

Figure 128 Irma celebrating her 106th birthday 111

Figure 129 George's questionably-acquired Kentucky Derby thoroughbred, Smokey. 112

Figure 130 Carina with her dog, Strider 113

Figure 131 Carina and David Mosier 114

Figure 132 Nicole Ana, through the years. 115

Figure 133 Year 1989 – Trip to Russia – Photo collage 116

Figure 134 Year 1989 – Trip to Russia – Mount Goryachaya, Pyatigorsk, Russia – The Eagle Monument - The Brass Eagle had sentimental value to my mother because she and her father took a picture in the same spot as we did, long ago 117

Figure 135 Year 1989 – Trip to Russia - Every night, we had young guys who would approach our table to talk to Lynne and bring flowers to all of the girls 118

Figure 136 Year 1989 – Trip to Russia - This show was put together specifically for American guests like us 118

Figure 137 Year 1989 – Trip to Russia – Strolling down Main Street 119

Figure 138 Year 1989 – Trip to Russia - Ana and I took a picture dressed up in traditional Russian outfits (don't mind the tennis shoes) 119

Figure 139 Year 1989 – Trip to Russia – Sheep and cows on the road in front of our van 120

Figure 140 Year 1989 – Trip to Russia – Hitchin' a ride with one of the locals 120

Figure 141 Traditional Russian dress 121

Figure 142 Iquitos, Peru 128

Figure 143 Peru 129

Figure 144 Lima, Peru 129

Figure 145 Year 2013 - Budapest, Hungary 130

Figure 146 Year 2014 – Gothenburg, Norway 130

Figure 147 Year 2017 - Bucharest, Romania 131

Figure 148 Madrid, Spain 131

Figure 149 Year 2015 – Vilnius, Lithuania 132

Figure 150 Year 2015 - Siauliai, Lithuania - "Land of the Crosses" - The first crosses were erected in 1831 in response to an uprising against Russian rule over the small Baltic country 132

Figure 151 As we traveled across Europe, we encountered poor beggars in every country. Thank God I was always on the giving end and not the receiving end 133

Figure 152 Amsterdam, Netherlands 133

Figure 153 Chile, South America 134

Figure 154 Year 2014 – Copenhagen, Denmark 134

Figure 155 Morocco, Africa 135

Figure 156 Cuba, North America 136

Figure 157 Cuba, North America - Nick and Brody 136

Figure 158 Cuba, North America - Notice that all of the books are mainly Cuban propaganda from the '50s and early 60s 137

Figure 159 Year 2012 - Alaska cruise 137

Figure 160 Year 2012 - Alaska cruise – George & Ana Lisenko 138

Figure 161 Year 2012 - Alaska cruise - George & Ana Lisenko 138

Figure 162 Year 2012 - Alaska cruise - Ana, Brenda, Marie, Patty (from left to right) 139

Figure 163 These are some of the parts that we made at Omni. 140

Figure 164 Newspaper article describing the FBI's sting operation, including the role that George played in the case. 144

Figure 165 The ring that George bought for Ana. 147

Figure 166 1969 Plymouth GTX 440 148

Figure 167 George Lisenko with 1969 Plymouth GTX 440 149

Figure 168 1969 Plymouth GTX 440 149

Figure 169 Political cartoon depicting corrupt politicians, which are mostly Democrats. 152

Figure 170 President Obama and Vice President Biden, who later became President, as well. 152

Figure 171 Corrupt politicians. 153

Figure 172 Donald Trump - 45th President of the United States of America - January 20, 2017 - January 20, 2021 - The Trump family: A true American success story 154

Figure 173 Small part of my gun collection 157

Figure 174 Gun shed 158

Figure 175 Pistol collection 159

Figure 176 WWII pistols 160

Figure 177 The Gun I'm holding is one of the Guns my Dad gave to his brother Johnny; the pistol is a P38 9mm FROM Walther arms, the main supplier of guns to the German Army during the war, my uncle says this gun is yours and is in his Will. 161

Figure 178 Part of my Trump Collection 162

Figure 179 Silver dollar coin collection. I'm missing 3 coins, the 1893-S, 94P, and 95P.............. 163

Figure 180 Part of my Silver collection (Marvel Comics) 164

Figure 181 Part of my USA Gold Collection 165

Figure 182 Part of my Gold Coin collection 166

Figure 183 Russian Silver Coins 167

Figure 184 Our Miniature Bottle Collection and Schaffer and Vater pieces (all made in Germany and over 100 years old – center cabinet) 168

Figure 185 Our Hard Rock Pin Collection representing over 100 countries 169

Figure 186 Part of my collection of signs 170

Figure 187 License Plates from 46 different United States and 51 from other countries so far that I have visited 171

Figure 188 Coca-Cola Sign, trash can, and bottle dispenser...172

Figure 189 This is an original 1930's scale 173

Figure 190 I MAY BE THE ONLY ONE that has a working phone booth in his backyard. As a matter of fact, I have two. I took the 2nd one to the shop and converted it into a shower. I had them both for over 30 years!..174

Figure 191 My 1915 cash register – This is the King of all Cash Registers..175

Figure 192 My jukeboxes 176

Figure 193 My new additions: Mobil Pegasus and Fire Chief Gas Pumps from the 1940s. Bought the Fire Chief Gas pump for Jonathan Hanna, my son-in-law, for he is a Fireman...177

Figure 194 One of my favorite pictures of my daughter Lynne 178

Figure 195 Ana and Angel, Brenda and Johnny, Manil and Sanjiv, Carlos and Angie, and friends having fun. Carlos, out of Chicago from Peru, has been my good friend for many years me, and him had lots of good times in my bottle collecting years. 179

Figure 196 Amy has been a good friend for over 30 years Beautiful then and Beautiful now. She sold me Metal for my shop she was and is in sells at the FRY STEEL CO. 180

Figure 197 Ana's friends Roxana and Lili...181

Figure 198 The Bonilla Family: Patty, Laura, and Yolanda (mom) 181

Figure 199 Bob and Patty – we have been friends for 38 years. Bob and Paddy had a very successful insurance business – Bob from New York and Paddy from Peru. She and Ana went to a Catholic school to together in Lima, Peru. 182

Figure 200 Our closest dear friends: Johnny and Brenda and their beautiful family and two of his cars. 182

Figure 201 Johnny, Brenda, and their kids. 183

Figure 202 My daughter Lynne, Debbie, Roxana, Carina, and John..184

Figure 203 George's cousin Albert Abda (son of John Abda, Jr.), and George 185

Figure 204 Lisa, Nancy, Albert, Joe, Johnny, Will, Diamond, and James (Love this picture)................186

Figure 205 James, William, Albert, Johnny, and Joe..186

Figure 206 (Left to right): Grandpa John, Grandma Diamond, and their five boys, Joseph, Johnny, William, Albert, and James...187

Figure 207 Lisa, Johnny, Nancy, Aaron, and Tara 188

Figure 208 Albert, Rosemary, Thea, Jim, Tara, Aaron, Dennis, John, Henry James 189

Figure 209 Johnny, Lisa, Al, Lynne, Jim, Denise, Alexis, and Nancy. 190

Figure 210 Tara's wedding day, with Aaron driving my dad's 1948 Chrysler. 191

Figure 211 Lenny and Lauren; John, Stephanie, Janis and Rene; Albert; Niki and Alex; Victor, Kim, Olga, and Jim; Our family; Lynne; Alexis, Richy, Denise; George, Ana, and Kathy; Melissa; Kaylan; Stephanie and kids 192

Figure 212 Lisa and Johnny; Albert and George; Lisa; Johnny, Albert, and kids 193

Figure 213 My picture as a Veteran was posted on the wall at the Veterans Administration Hospital in Long Beach, CA. Where the hell did all the years go? As my mom used to say, it SUCKS getting older. Boy, ain't that the truth? 194

Figure 214 Ronny, Jimmy, and Richard; John, Rene, Janis and Stephanie; Sandra and Jay; Ashley and Lauren; The Davis Family, Lenny, and Denise; The Lisenko family; Erica, Galina, and Rebecca; Jim and Olga; Melissa and Christina 195

Figure 215 William, Joe, Johnny, James, and Albert.. 196

Figure 216 George and Lenny 197

Figure 217 Ana and George.. 197

Figure 218 Alex, Niki, Ana, and George 198

Figure 219 Righteous Brothers Concert – Ana, George, Maria, Bill Medley, Brenda, Johnny, and Javier (2010).. 199

Figure 220 Niki 200

Figure 221 Alex 201

Figure 222 Niki 202

Figure 223 Our Family picture.. 203

Figure 224 Niki and her friends are out having a good time in Texas..................... 203

Figure 225 My NIKI is fully loaded. All 5 of my kids love Guns. I guess it helps to be very Conserved. I took my kids out to the desert at an early age to go shooting, and they loved it. 204

Figure 226 Uncle Johnny and George... 204

Figure 227 .45 caliber 1911 that Albert Abda brought home from WWII. 205

Figure 228 My son Lenny pictures 206

Figure 229 Lenny, his Mom Lelah, and Lynne.. 207

Figure 230 Lenny and his Beautiful wife Denise.. 208

Figure 231 Lynne and Lenny 209

Figure 232 Denise and Lenny's wedding day... 210

Figure 233 Denise and Lenny saying their wedding vows 211

Figure 234 Denise and Lenny's wedding reception.. 212

Figure 235 Lenny's daughter Lauren and Smokey, our family horse, have been with us for 35 years....213

Figure 236 Me and my beautiful granddaughter Lauren 214

Figure 237 Sister Olga and family 215

Figure 238 My brother Victor and family... 216

Figure 239 My sister Frieda and family (with Aunt Nina) 217

Figure 240 My sister Denise and family 218

Figure 241 My sister Alexis and family and my dad's 1948 Town and Country Chrysler, bottom picture with Uncle Johnny. 219

Figure 242 My two sisters came to visit California, and with Ana, they are enjoying the jacuzzi. 220

Figure 243   The Davis and Nahal families are so happy to be part of these Beautiful Families! 221

Figure 244 David Mosier and his granddaughters, Fiona and Olivia. 222

Figure 245 Lisa The Crazy Dog Lady is one of my first Cousins and one of my favorites; she is a very hard-working dog groomer and provides herself a very good livening and is fun to B.S. with. 223

Figure 246 Sandra King (Abda), her husband Jay King, and their kids 224

Figure 247 Cousins Richard and Lauren (Richard was the first cousin I met that came to California)....225

Figure 248 Uncle Johnny's 3 kids, Rene, Stephanie, and John, ...226

Figure 249 My grandson, Trevor Goldyn 227

Figure 250 Trevor in USMC uniform 228

Figure 251 Trevor on active duty and as a senior in high school 228

Figure 252 Abda family 229

Figure 253 My first cousin Sandra and her husband Jay, who sadly passed away. 230

Figure 254 My cousin Richard with my niece Ashley on her wedding day 231

Figure 255 Uncle Johnny and I visiting Abda's graves in Scranton, PA..232

Figure 256 Abda's uncles and Grandma Diamond. 232

Figure 257 Jim and Alexis at their wedding 238

Figure 258 Jim and Alexis's wedding reception..239

Figure 259 The Christening gowns! Henry and Mason in the gown and slip made by the cloister nuns. 240

Figure 260 This is me in front of my grandparent's home in Wanamassa, New Jersey.........................241

Figure 261 My mom and her grandmother in front of our church, St. Joseph's Melkite, in Scranton, PA

....242

Figure 262 Year 1958 - Christmas in Scranton, PA..243

Figure 263 Dad, the butcher! 243

Figure 264 Alexis and I..244

Figure 265 My favorite room in the house my dad built 245

Figure 266 The Monte Carlo in Ashbury Park, NJ 246

Figure 267 Jim and Alexis with their children, Thea, John, Aaron, and Tara 247

Figure 268 An incredible New York-style department store 247

Figure 269 From left to right - Foster & Bertha Dennis, Diamond & John Abda – Picture was taken on our parents' wedding day..248

Figure 270 Diamond, on the far right, with her 8 sisters, and her mother is front and center 249

Figure 271 Grandpa and Granny Abda, along with their five sons: Joseph, William, Albert, James, and John, who all lived in or around Scranton. 250

Figure 272 I bought my wedding dress at the Globe store, of course..251

Figure 273 Henry's Parents Henry and Marjorie Nahal, on their 50th Wedding anniversary..................252

Figure 274 Our blessing in life 253

Dedication

Acknowledgements

About the Author

Nina, Galina, and Freida Meet Albert and George

The older I get, the more I find that I should put my life on paper for my grandkids to know some things about me.

Let's see now; I was born on October 1, 1946, and I guess you can call me a war baby or a baby boomer. My mother, Galina Lisenko, was born in Russia in 1925 in a small town named Pyatigorsk.

Year 1946 - Galina Lisenko (my mother)

Her mother, Nina Kruger, was born in Riga, Latvia, and was half Russian and half German. When my mother was approximately 8 years old, her mother passed away. Her father, George Lisenko, changed his last name from Lisenkoff (Russian) to Lisenko (Ukrainian) in the 1930s due to the Stalin Purges. The Stalin Purges was a brutal campaign led by Soviet dictator Joseph Stalin to eliminate political enemies. During these purges, at least 750,000 people were executed, and more than 1,000,000 people were sent to Gulags or forced labor camps. Gramps was an anti-communist, so he had to be very careful not to get himself killed.

Year 1945 - My mom, Galina, holding my dad's .45 pistol

My father, Albert M. Abda, was born on November 22, 1923, in Scranton, PA. He was of Lebanese descent and was one of 5 brothers: Joe (the salesman), William (the grocery store owner), James (the police officer), the youngest Johnny (the doctor), and my father Albert (self-employed). My father, Albert, joined the U.S. Army and was sent to Germany to fight the Nazis.

Year 1945 - Albert Abda (my father)

In Germany, Mom worked as an assistant to the nurses and doctors in the hospitals. On July 27, 1944, my sister, Elfriede Lisenko, was born in Untermerzbach, Germany. Elfriede later changed her name to Frieda when she became a U.S. citizen. After the war, Heinz and my mother realized that they hardly knew each other, and having a child was difficult, so they parted ways. In 1945, my mother met an American Soldier named Albert Abda, and they fell in love.

Year 1945 - Albert Abda and Galina Lisenko

Eventually, Hitler invaded Poland and some of the neighboring countries, and it was just a matter of time before he invaded Russia. My Grandfather joined the Russian Army, but once he saw how the Russians treated their own troops and his own brother who was wounded (where gangrene set in and they simply let him die), he decided that this was enough for him, and he deserted the Russian Army in order to join the German Army. However, once joining the German Army, he saw how they treated the Russians and the civilians. Soldiers in the German Army raped women, hung civilians, burned down whole villages with people in them, etc. Once again, he deserted the Germans and left one more time. My mother and her father immigrated to Germany in 1943. The Germans treated the refugees (displaced persons, or D.P.s) a lot better if they had any German blood in them, as my grandmother did. Therefore, she was treated better than the refugees.

Mom went through hell, as the allies were bombing Germany both day and night until GERMANY WAS FINALLY BROUGHT TO ITS KNEES! Mom and gramps moved from one refugee camp, and one soup line, to another.

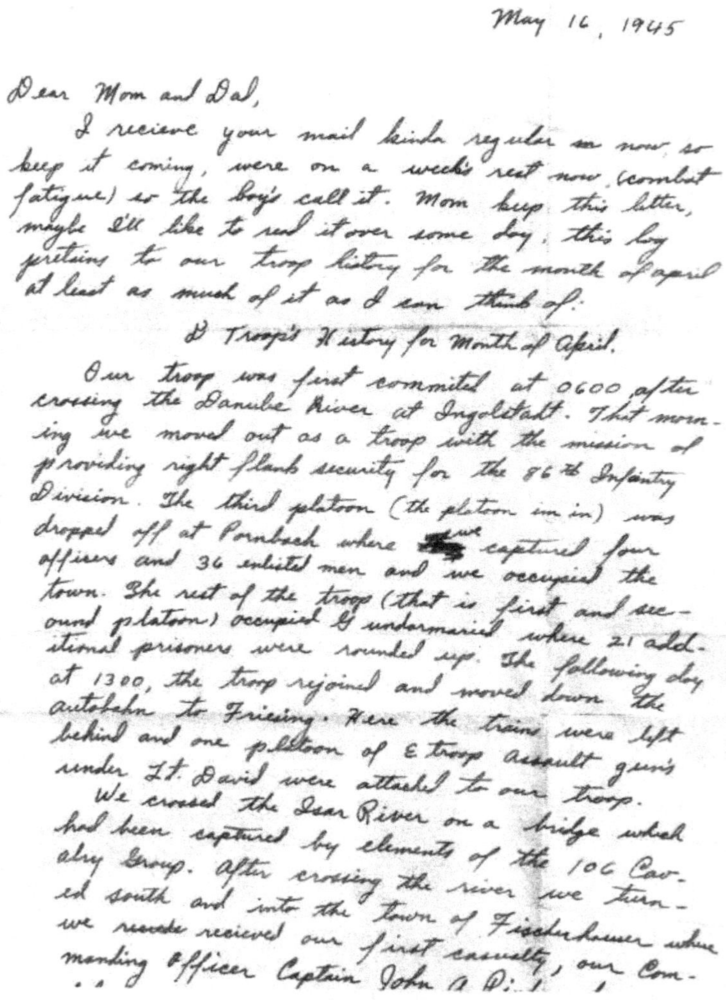

Figure 1 Year 1945 - Albert Abda letters to his parents (1 of 2)

of the sniper's was wounded by our platoon leader Lt. Warr and the other captured, how many other's we killed I don't know, I guess there wasn't a gun silenced for twenty minutes. Orders were issued at that time that there would be no more prisoners taken, these orders were issued by Lt. Burke who assumed command of the troop since Captain Pindi's wound was too serious to continue and he was evacuated to the rear. After clearing all enemy opposition we moved south to Ismaning, where we cleared out some remaining sniper's, the snipers usually consisted of S.S. men whom we only dealt in death term's. We then swung northeast to Zengenoos and on to Moosinning where approximately 100 Krauts were deployed against elements of the 106 Cavalry, after they killed a few they come out like rats, two of the S.S. men who were captured had killed several of their own men who wanted to surrender. From there we went to Nieder Neuching and crossed the Isar Canal which had been under enemy artillery fire fifteen minutes prior to our arrival, we continued north to Reissing where we set up out posts and rested for the night (which was very unusual). This totalled our actions for the month of April.

I have to get the names of a few more towns before I could write about the happenings in May, we really had six days of hell on earth from may 1 to may 6 Ill write another chapter on may soon.
Bill should I . ...

Figure 2 Year 1945 - Albert Abda letter to his parents (2 of 2)

Albert met my mother during his enlistment in the Army. As my mother puts it, she fell in love with my father, Albert, at first sight. Albert and his mother spent as much time together as they could. Albert was constantly bringing her food and whatever he could to help her. Mom said he was somewhat of a wheeler-and-dealer as well as a hustler and always came up with lots of stuff. They went to church every Sunday in a small town named Dettelbach.

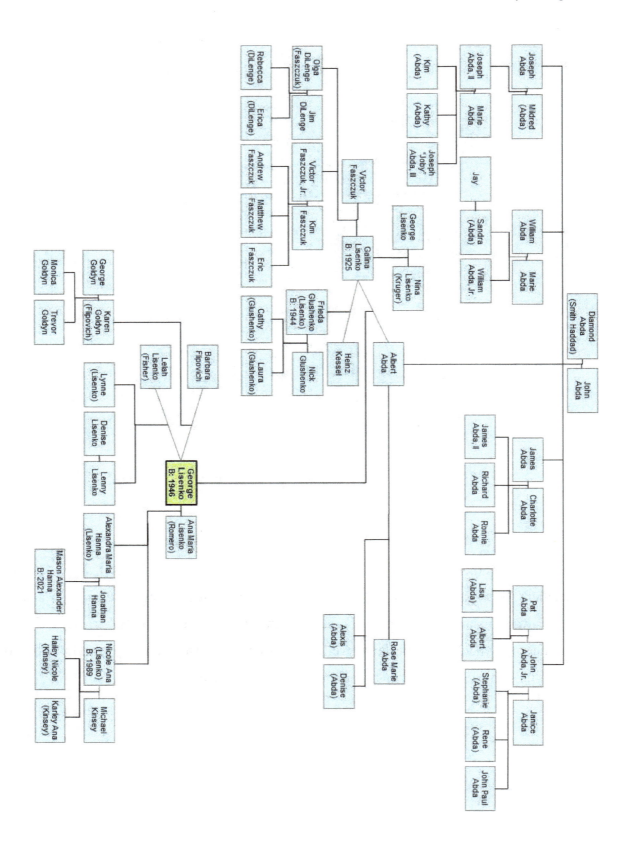

Figure 3 Family tree descending from John and Diamond Abda

Early Life: Emigrants and Netherlands

As the war ended, things improved a little, and my mother became pregnant sometime around the end of January 1945. I'm not sure when, but my father was rotated back to the States. Before he left, he gave my mother a ring and promised her that he would send for us and bring us back to Scranton, PA. However, that was not to be. My father gave my mother his mother's (Granny Abda's) diamond and her address in Scranton, PA. My mother waited and waited and finally gave up on Albert. In the early 1950s, my sister and I were sent to Holland, the Netherlands, where I stayed at a farmhouse and Frieda stayed with a priest. I remember asking myself, "Why did my mom give my sister and me away?" It turned out that the Queen of the Netherlands had a program in place to help refugee families, so we were sent to Holland for 3 consecutive years for two months at a time to the same families. I clearly remember a couple making out in a barn, and the guy stood up, gave me a few pennies, and told me to "PISS OFF!" All I remember is that they were both naked. At the time, I had no idea why.

In 1954 we lived in Erlangen, Germany. My mother was single with 2 kids and qualified for a program where underprivileged kids were given the opportunity to spend a summer with families in the Netherlands. My sister, Frieda, and I were sent by train to a city named Hilversum with several other children. Once we arrived in Hilversum, we were split up, and she went to stay with Pastor Smith and his family while I was put on a farm with the Versteh family. During that visit, on June 14, 1954, the entire group of underprivileged kids were brought to Naarden, Netherlands, to visit the grounds of the Castle where Queen Wilhelmina reigned.

There, the future Queen Julianna (daughter of Queen Wilhelmina) presented us with a blue Kerchief depicting red tulips (the national flower) and a family walking in wooden shoes. It had the date imprinted on it, thus making it very special to each of us. In June 1954, while we were in the Netherlands, my mom married Victor Faszczuk. My sister, Olga, was born on March 10, 1955.

Figure 4 Year 1954 - Queen Wilhelmina –The Netherlands - She handed out blue handkerchiefs to all the kids and my sister and I still have ours.

Figure 5 Olga, Mom, Victor, and Yura (Victor II). Once my sister and I were gone, they were one happy family.

Victor Faszczuk, my stepfather, worked in the kitchen of the American Soldiers Camp in Erlangen. He was able to bring home some leftover food, sometimes meat, but mostly chocolate bars. We were able to trade the chocolate bars for money from the German children, which gave us the opportunity to buy items we otherwise wouldn't have been able to obtain.

They were finally approved. Mom and victor gained their citizenship the legal way, not like today, where you can just walk across the border and get free shit (thanks to Traitor Joe and his followers). Mom and Victor had to sign an abundance of paperwork stating that they would not accept any money from the government or help of any kind. UNFORTUNATELY, that is not how it works today!

Coming to America

On February 22, 1957, we were finally given permission to immigrate to the USA after being on the waiting list for four years. Grandfather George was rejected by the U.S. authorities because they found a benign spot on his lung, so he didn't come with us. Victor's father, Roman, had immigrated a few years earlier to Chicago, IL. He became our sponsor, providing a job for both Mom and Dad and a partially furnished apartment on Campbell Ave. and Cortez St.

Figure 6 Year 1957 – Campbell Ave. and Cortez St. – Chicago, IL – The first place we lived coming from Germany - 2nd floor left where there a Bears banner is.

We were the first refugees to come to the USA by plane, as all of the refugees before us came by ship. I remember landing in Canada and carrying Olga down the stairs of the plane. As I sat her down on the ground, she disappeared into the snow. From there, we went to Ellis Island, a federally owned island in New York. The two most famous inspection stations were New York's Ellis Island (1892 – 1957) and San Francisco's Angel Island (1910 - 1940). New York was the busiest port, receiving up to 5 million immigrants in a single year. My mother smoked, and I remember looking down at the ground and picking up a cigarette butt (which was bigger compared to the cigarette butts in Germany) and handing it to Mom, where she said to me in Russian, "Put that down, we are not in Germany but in America." I also clearly remember Victor saying to me, "If you can't talk in Ukrainian, then don't talk at all!" I clearly remember looking up at the sky scrapers as a 10-year-old, and it was something I just can't explain. From New York, we boarded a train to Chicago, where we met with Nina, Victor's sister. She took us to our apartment building, which was a few blocks away from where she lived.

Mom and Victor worked long and hard hours to make ends meet. Mom got a job in a factory, and Victor got a job as a machinist. Little did I know, that brought us one step closer to my father, Albert.

However, Victor had a bad habit of hitting the bottle on the weekends. How he managed to crawl home, just to wake up two to three hours later on Saturday mornings to leave for work, I'll never know, but he did. I was in 5th grade in Germany, but somehow, I ended up in 3rd grade in America. School and I never did see eye to eye. I suppose because I did not speak English. In school, I started becoming interested in girls and music.

Figure 7 Year 1957 - Frederic Chopin Elementary School – Chicago, IL

Growing Up: Melting Into the Pot

As I turned 11 years old, I started to ask more and more about my dad. However, my mom wasn't giving me much information. When I turned 12 years old, I began watching the 3 Stooges while Fritz was into American Bandstand.

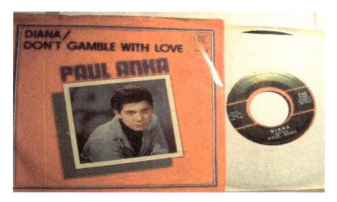

Figure 8 Year 1957 – Paul Anka

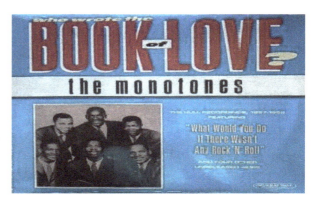

Figure 9 Year 1958 – The Monotones

Figure 10 Year 1958 – Danny and the Juniors

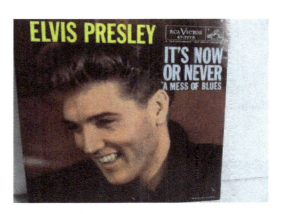

Figure 12 Year 1960 – Elvis Presley

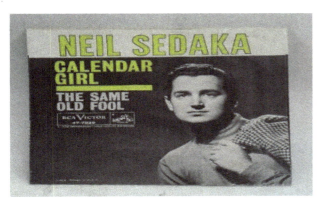

Figure 11 Year 1960 – Neil Sedaka

Figure 13 Year 1960 – Steve Lawrence

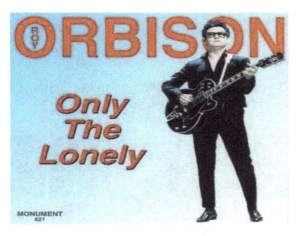

Figure 14 Year 1961 – Roy Orbison

Figure 17 Year 1963 – The Ronettes

Figure 15 Year 1961 - Jarmels

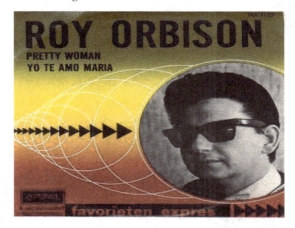

Figure 18 Year 1964 – Roy Orbison

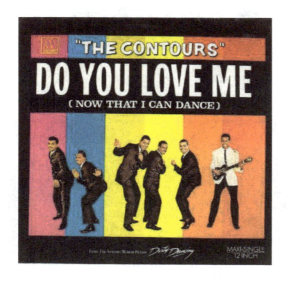

Figure 16 Year 1962 – The Contours

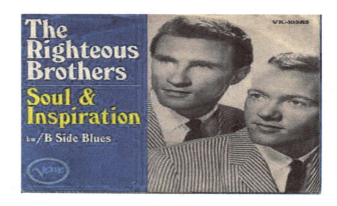

Figure 19 Year 1965 – The Righteous Brothers

Figure 20 Year 1960 – Marty Robbins

Figure 24 Year 1962 – The 4 Seasons

Figure 21 Year 1959 - Dion

Figure 25 Year 1965 – The Vogues

Figure 22 Year 1960 – Marty Robbins

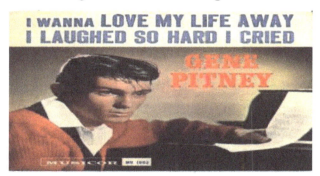

Figure 26 Year 1961 – Gene Pitney

Figure 23 Year 1964 – Four Tops

Figure 27 Year 1961 – The Tokens

All of these record sleeve pictures have special meaning for each of the years they are listed, as they remind me of some meaningful event or some girl that I met that year.

By then, I had my first girlfriend, Darlene. It just didn't feel right, her being two years ahead of me in school, but we got along regardless. I did not like being called a D.P. (displaced person), so I decided to stop speaking Russian, German, and Ukrainian and start speaking English in order to become an American boy.

Crime Times

At the age of 13, I started to get into trouble. I was tired of being picked on, so I joined a gang called Chi-West (a Ukrainian gang, sometimes referred to as the "Ukrainian Mafia"), which stood for Chicago and Western (my neighborhood at the time). There were lots of gangs in Chicago, like the C-Notes (an Italian gang), the Black Rangers (which we called "The Shines" who prevailed in the Puerto Rican area on the north-west side), the Vice Lords (who prevailed in the south side and the west side), and the Mexican gangs like the Latin Counts.

Figure 28 Year 1963 – Chicago and Western Gang (my gang)

At the age of 14, I pressed my mom a bit harder for information about my father, and she began to open up and tell me about him. She disclosed that my father and his family were from Syria (I remember thinking, "Oh shit, I'm a rag-head or a camel-jockey.") Later, I found out that my father was of Lebanese descent, and his family immigrated to the states in the late 1800s.

As time passed, I started to get in trouble more and more. In high school, I dropped a cherry bomb into the bathroom toilet and blew it out. Why? I suppose because it was something fun to do at the time. Around this time, I determined that I needed a bike, but I knew better than to ask my mom, so I simply stole one. Eventually, my mom left Victor (she was the one who initiated the process). She left him a chair, a coffee table, and some pots and pans to cook with. My mom moved us to Iowa St. in Chicago, IL. My mom eventually asked me if she should take Victor back, and I replied, "Mom, it's your call, not mine, and I will be joining the Marines as soon as I am of age.

You are the one who will live with him and not me." My mom ended up taking Victor back, and he continued to hit the bottle on the weekends.

Some things I did "just because" – I ordered a half-dozen pizzas to be delivered to a house where I just didn't like the guy. A few days later, I called in a false fire alarm. A few weeks later, I called in an emergency and claimed that the guy had a heart attack. A month or so later, my fellow friends in crime and I got a bag and filled it up with dog shit, lit it on fire, rang the doorbell, ran across the street, and watched the guy stomp on the bag of shit. Why? I guess it was just something to do at the time. I got into more and more gang fights. When my mom told me my dad smoked Camel cigarettes, I started to smoke them. Looking back, it was the worst habit I ever picked up.

I got my first job at Jack's Red Hots, where I made $40.00 a week and gave my mom half of the money. Jack was a good guy, but when he stepped out of the store, I would invite my friends over for some free dogs.

I also had a job where I was making, of all things, holy crosses. I had to take the Chicago L train ("L" is short for "elevated") from my home in Chicago, IL, to Oak Park, IL. I had to transfer from one train to another in a black neighborhood, which was scary, to say the least.

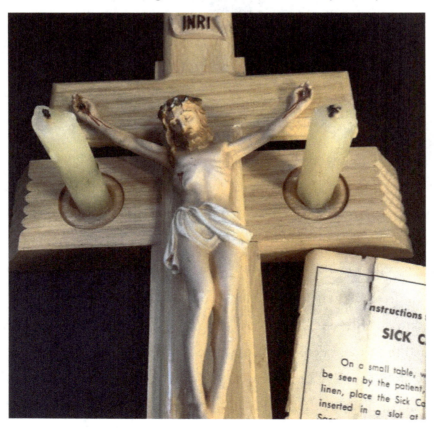

Figure 29 The types of crosses I made

On November 23, 1963, I was at work when my boss told me that our 35th president, John F. Kennedy, was killed. I was NOT a Kennedy fan, but that was a very, very sad day.

Figure 30 Year 1963 - John F. Kennedy, the 35th President of the United States, sitting with his wife, Jacqueline Kennedy. He was shot in the head while riding in a motorcade in Dallas, Texas, on November 22, 1963

I remember that in 1960 when I was 11 years old, I found out that my mom had voted for Richard Nixon. I asked my mom, "What is the difference between a Democrat and a Republican?" She replied, "Well, Son, if you feel like someone owes you something and you have your hand out and are just plain lazy, you will automatically be a Democrat. However, if you don't mind hard work and you don't want anything from anyone, then you will automatically be a Republican." Once I turned 18, I started voting and voted Republican during every election. I loved our 37th President, Richard Nixon, who served our country from 1969 – 1974. I feel that President Nixon was really screwed over by the Democrats since he won his 2nd presidential term by a huge landslide, yet somehow a handful of liberals had him removed from office? I also loved our 40th U.S. President, Ronald Reagan, who served our country from 1981 – 1989.

At the age of 14, I started making pipe bombs. It was very easy to make: you get a 4" x 4" threaded (1" round) on both ends, get two caps, and drill a small hole in one end for the wick. Then, you buy a box of matches for a nickel, get a pair of scissors, cut off the red tips of the matches, and stuff them into the pipe as tight as possible. Then, you screw the cap on and insert the wick, and you have one hell of a bomb. My favorite thing to do was to do the same thing with a CO-2 cartridge, where I would tape it to the inside of a car window, stick the fuse in halfway, and light a cigarette butt (which would give me plenty of time to get away). The results were always the same – the window would be completely blown out. Why? It was just something to do. I remember once, just as I lit the fuse in a car, I saw a cop car on Western Ave. between two buildings. I remember thinking, "Oh shit, they are going to turn down our way." They did. At the time, there were 8 or 9 of us, and as the cop car turned toward us, I ran toward the cop car while the others ran away from it. I remember thinking that the two cops would give chase to the others. However, I was wrong; the cop car stopped, and one cop ran after me. I turned the corner and ran into the hallway of a 3-story building, and the cop followed me. I heard him say, "You better get your fucking ass down here before I put a bullet up your ass." Right when he said that, I heard the car's windshield blow out, and I decided that I would not be surrendering. I opened the hallway window, and since it was December, it was around 5 degrees outside. I jumped out onto the building next to it, slid down the side, grabbed the drain pipe, and took it with me as I fell down. Somehow, I managed to get up, ran across Western Ave., darted into an alleyway, crawled into a garbage can, and closed the lid.

As I turned 16 years old, I had 4 different girlfriends. On a warm Chicago night, my friends and I liked to walk around the neighborhood looking for open windows to throw a few M-80s into. Looking back now, that must have been one rude way to wake up. I often think back and wonder, "Who thinks of these things?" I guess the answer is, "I did." By now, things were getting pretty bad with Victor and my mom. I remember asking my mom one day, "What is that hole in the kitchen wall?" Finally, she disclosed that Victor had thrown a knife at her. That evening, I told Victor, "I will kill you if you ever touch my mom again!" He knew the type of friends that I hung out with, so that was that. He once called the cops on me; it seems he found my sword, Billy club, and some flares, which he thought were dynamite. I remember the cop; the cop said, "Nice sword. Why did he call the cops on you?" I simply responded, "He was a sick old man." I'm SURE the cop took my stuff home with him!

Once, a big Polack was giving my girlfriend a hard time, so I told him, "Let's get it on!" and he just laughed at me. Even though he was much bigger than me, I had a plan: I had a roll of nickels in my fist. The plan worked pretty well; as soon as he started to take off his leather jacket and his hands were behind his back, I hit him as hard as I could, and he dropped like a brick and was out like a light. As he slowly got up, I told him, "The next time you fuck with my girl, I'll use this Zip gun on you. Just try me!" That was the end of that.

As we moved to Iowa St., we ended up moving next door to Sara. She had the biggest boobs in school, so I quickly made the moves on her.

Figure 31 Year 1963 – George Lisenko

Sometime in 1963, my friend Mike and I took his dad's Rag Top (1962 Ford convertible), and we took off to go to a drive-in movie. We ran into 3 girls that had just moved down from Joplin, IL. There was: Lana Love-in, Marylyn Holt, and Marylyn's sister. We hit it off, as it seems that they were as bad as we were. One of our favorite things to do at the time was to go to different restaurants, order something expensive, and then slowly perform our disappearing act where I would crawl out of the bathroom window (they were on their own to escape however they saw fit). We did lots of shopping together. But why not? It was all free! I don't remember ever getting caught. We had some good times together. Some days we slept together on the floor and did our little thing together. Eventually, the three girls ended up getting a job together, working for some nut house in a small town outside of Chicago.

Half a block away from where I lived, on the corner of Western Ave. and Iowa St., there was a car lot called See Eddy's Used Cars. Mike, Clarence, and I piled into a 1953 Chevy Bel-Air, and we quickly started it up. Mike got behind the wheel, and I jumped out and dropped the chain, got back in the car, and we took off on a joy ride. It turned out to be one hell of an adventure. Gas was cheap at that time at $0.27 per gallon.

Figure 32 Year 1953 – Chevy Bel-Air

Figure 33 Year 1963 – Gas Prices

    I don't think we had a dollar between us. We headed out of the city limits and ended up in St. Charles, IL, on some lonely road. We figured that we would continue driving the car as far as we could until we ran out of gas, which finally happened around 3:00 AM. It was jet black out there, and we had no clue where we were. I heard what sounded to me like cow bells, so I thought, "Where there are cows, there must be a farm house nearby." We followed the sounds of the cow bells until we ran into some barbed wire. I had a feeling that this was an electric wire, so I asked

Clarence to hold the wire open so that Mike and I could go through it, and then I would hold the wire open for him to step through. As he grabbed the wire, he got the shock of his life, and it took a while for him to get his shit together. By then, it must have been somewhere around morning time. Sure enough, we started running into lots of cows. The sun started to come up as we approached the front door, and I remember thinking, "Some fried eggs and bacon will do just fine." Well, that was just wishful thinking on my part. The house light was already on as I rang the doorbell, and a farmer and his 15-year-old kid answered the door. I told them that we ran out of gas, and I was wondering if we could buy some gas from them and whether it would be possible to get something to eat from them. He gave us 3 green apples and told his son to give us a ride to the car on his tractor, and so he did. I am not sure why, but when we got back to our car and tried putting gas into it, it wouldn't start. We asked the kid to give us a push (back then, a car would start with a push), and the kid said, "I can't because the tractor will crush the trunk." I told the kid, "So what? It's my car. Just do it." The kid gave the car a push, the car started up, and my friends and I took off. I can still hear the kid yelling, "Hey, the gas money!" Little did he know that we didn't have any money. On the way back, although we shared the driving, Mike was the oldest and did most of the driving. It was close to 6:00 AM when we got a flat tire in the rear of the car, and we pulled over to see if we had a spare. We didn't have the keys to the car to unlock the trunk, so we went through the back seat just to find out we had no spare tire. We decided to get as close to Chicago as we could and then abandon the car and hitchhike back. Soon enough, the rear tire had burnt off, and we were riding on the brake drum. There were sparks flying everywhere and the back seat was full of smoke.

St. Charles was a very small town. If I remember correctly, there was only one light in the whole town. As we drove closer to the light, Mike slammed on the brakes. However, the problem was that there were no brakes since we had been riding on the drum for so long. The traffic light turned red, and there was a lady in the crosswalk and a cop car on the opposite side. Mike had one choice: to swerve to avoid the lady. In doing so, he crashed into a pole and a Cadillac. The car burst into flames, and Mike and I took off, running as fast as we could. We entered into a lumber yard and started to crawl up the fence but soon heard a cop yell, "Get your ass down here before I but some buckshot up your ass." As we walked toward the cop car, we saw Clarence in the back seat. I will never forget the jail where we ended up, as it was a huge barn that had horses and a fire station. The jail itself had four walls which were all made of iron bars, and an abundance of straw covered the floor. Next thing we knew, we were on our way to Joliet State Prison. Once we arrived at the prison, we did some paperwork, and I remember lying about my age so that I wasn't separated from my friends. This turned out to be a huge mistake (too much to talk about), as I began to realize that I was locked up with some really bad people like kidnappers, killers, child molesters, blacks, Puerto Ricans, and more. I remember, clearly, that when the cafeteria gates unlocked, you only had a few minutes to enter the eating hall before they locked the gates again. I did not enter fast enough, and I got locked out. At the next meal, I made sure to go through the gates in time. In the eating hall, there was a large steel table to eat on. One big naked black guy was walking up and down the table, and no one dared to look up. I said to myself, "I need to get the FUCK out of here." I called for the guard so that I could tell him that I was only 16 years old and I didn't belong there, but my claims fell on deaf ears. 11 days passed before my mom got me out of jail.

Figure 34 Year 1964 – My time

When I was 17 years old, things got even worse. I started robbing places along with some of the members of my gang. When we were in the process of robbing places, I would tell my fellow accomplices, "Ok, I'm in. I got a hold of a 12-gauge shotgun." I told my accomplices not to carry any live ammo. One guy had a .38 hand gun, and the other had a Billy club. We entered a Chinese grocery store, and I was carrying a sawed-off shotgun under my leather jacket. Larry told the grocery store clerk, "Open the fucking register!" However, the owner just stood there, silent and confused. Larry repeated, "Open the fucking register!" As it turned out, the owner of the Chinese grocery store didn't speak English. We knocked the register off the table, and as the register hit the ground, it opened up. I don't think there was more than $80.00 in it, so it was not much of a haul, but Larry filled his leather jacket with the last of the candy bars and Twinkies. During this time, I also started to snatch purses from poor little old ladies. In addition, some of my friends and I started crashing the wedding parties of strangers, just for something fun to do. We would get free food and also have the opportunity to meet and dance with new girls. When they asked me who I was related to, I simply pointed to some old man. I remember standing next to a large table with a 3-layer cake when I noticed two stacks of what looked like silver dollars. I looked around, and when I had the chance, I grabbed both of the stacks and put them in my leather jacket pockets - cake and all. I shot out of there and left my friends behind. I could hardly believe my eyes – two stacks of 25 silver dollars! 50 big ones! Wow, what a haul! I didn't realize at the time that it was someone's 50th anniversary! While there, I met a girl named Barbara. I guess you could say that I started to see her a lot. Her mother was a waitress, so she was not home often, and Barbara and I had a lot of time alone with each other. The next thing I knew, Barbara was pregnant.

Time to Be a Soldier

My 8 friends and I decided to join the Marines; we all wanted to join the best of the best. Since I grew up in a bad neighborhood where crime was a way of life, and most of my friends ended up in jail, I decided that this was the best decision. Back then, there was this idea that you had to join the Marines or you weren't shit. Of my gang of 12, 11 of us joined the Marines, and only 1 of us joined the Army. Most did not return. I remember being in front of a judge where he told me, "I understand you have joined the Marines, so here is the way I see it: You are going to do some time for me one way or another. The question is, will it be above me or below me! If you go into the Marines, you are off the hook. If you don't, you are going to jail, and that's that!" I felt very bad for Barbara, but I was committed to the Marines, so I asked my friend Mike to keep an eye on her. The Marine recruiter kept telling me to stay out of trouble for a few months. I had already passed all of my tests, so I did my best to do what my recruiter had suggested. I finally received the call to be at the downtown recruiting office on December 24, 1964. I was 17 years old. I guess the quota was low, so they took me.

Figure 35 Year 1965 – I started boot camp in San Diego, CA, in January of 1965. My life was completely turned around, that's for sure, as it became a series of "Yes, sirs" and "No, sirs".

Figure 36 George Lisenko sitting down with a gun

Figure 37 Year 1966 - Guard Roster

However, now, I had a place to stay and 3 meals a day. I spent 8 weeks at boot camp and 4 weeks at the rifle range at Camp Pendleton. I was in 1st Battalion, 3rd Marines Fleet Marine Force, Pacific. I was a grunt 0311 infantryman, 60mm mortars, and M-14 rifleman, as well as a grenadier 79mm.

Figure 38 Just out of Boot Camp with my Marine friends visiting Tijuana, Mexico in 1965 – Me, George Lange, Danny Rudd, and several other friends

I boarded the ship, USS Mitchell, in San Diego, CA, and we stopped first in Hawaii. Then, we headed to Okinawa for jungle training, where I was also assigned to an Army base to attend Vietnamese language school. Unfortunately, I never learned the Vietnamese language. After leaving Honolulu, Hawaii, we headed for Okinawa. On the way to Okinawa, we hit a typhoon. Our ship felt like a toothpick in the ocean waves. We had like 5,000 marines on board, and it seems like 85% of the Marines were sea sick and throwing up. We were not allowed to open the doors to the deck, for the waves were gigantic and went over the ship… but I managed to crack a door slightly, and soon as I had the air in my face, it helped me not get sick. The ship was extremely crowded, and we slept in bunk beds 5 high unless we were skinny. It was hard to get through the aisles. I personally preferred to sleep on top, for the smell was too hard to handle. We were issued life jackets at the time. No one paid much attention to it, but when the typhoon hit, everyone was scrambling to get our hands on one, including me. Prior to getting on the ship, we read an article in a newspaper that said that the Psychic who predicted Kennedy's assassination predicted that the USS Mitchell would hit a typhoon and sink. This was one of the scariest moments in my life. It was difficult to imagine sinking. However, we survived the typhoon. Afterward, we stopped in Japan, and then we finally ended up in Vietnam.

Figure 39 Six of my friends from my squad

Figure 40 Camp Hansen, Okinawa

Figure 41 Aiming a grenade launcher

We were told that Naha, Okinawa was off-limits, so we all headed for Naha to spend our last days in titty bars before heading to Vietnam. Why? It was just something to do!

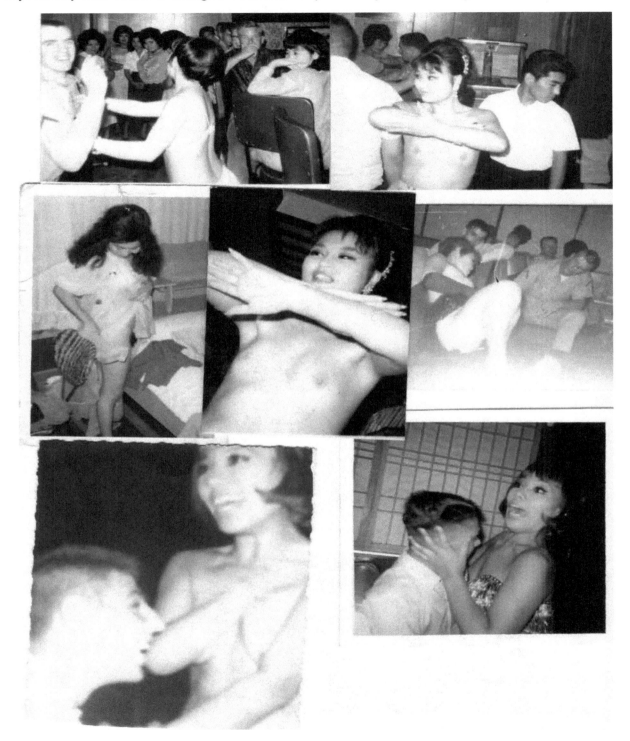

Figure 42 Last days in Naha, Okinawa, before shipping to Vietnam. Me (bottom left picture) and my good friend, John, who I called E.J. (bottom right picture)

Vietnam Era

Figure 43 Badges for George's USMC teams

I was sent to Vietnam, a place I knew nothing about. As a matter of fact, I didn't even know where Vietnam was, let alone what the Vietnamese looked like.

Figure 44 Life on ship. Tight quarters, muster drills, all of your possessions in a duffel bag, and sleeping racks stacked five high.

We made a World War II-style landing in Red Beach, Da Nang. All of the Marines were nervous and ready to shoot. The problem was that we didn't know who or what to shoot at.

Figure 45 Helo transport picking up troops in a rice paddy

On our first day, General Westmoreland (Commander of all U.S. forces) gave us a speech. I remember that it was hotter than hell, and the next day, monsoon rain poured down on us. I believe that it rained for 3 months straight, day and night, where we were drenched to the skin constantly in the mud-flooded jungle. It was pure misery. We encountered blood-sucking leeches, foot-long rats, and giant snakes, and who could forget about the giant mosquitoes everywhere we went?

Figure 46 Giant snakes, rats, centipedes, mosquitoes. It seemed like this was an every-day-type thing

Additionally, we also heard the sound of heavy artillery 24-7; death and destruction were everywhere.

Figure 47 Troop life in Viet Nam involved a lot of marching and vigilance. Vietnamese currency and political cartoons (right).

Figure 48 U.S. tank moving across a field. Air strike visible on the horizon.

At night, we were sent out to set up a night ambush against the Viet Cong (we called them "V-C" or "Charlie"). We would sit there in the dead of night until we heard "Charlie" in attack range. Then, we would open fire and hope we made it back to our base camp in one piece. As a Marine, we are committed to "kill or be killed."

Figure 49 Some of the traps the Viet Cong laid for us

Figure 50 It was a big deal to have a body count for the Top Brass

Figure 51 Another body count for the Top Brass. It was very sad, but this is the way it was. This is what I saw when I first arrived.

Figure 52 Viet Cong prisoners of war

Figure 53 Viet Cong spiked booby trap

Figure 54 Explosions and fires as the war was fought near Vietnamese villages

Figure 55 Various bathing situations during the war

Figure 56 U.S. troops landing at a Vietnamese beach

Figure 57 Eating VFC (Vietnam Fried Chicken)

Figure 58 Artillery

Figure 59 Medics tending to a wounded soldier

Figure 60 Helicopter troop transports, artillery, and support aircraft

Figure 61 Armor units arriving via boat

Figure 62 Burning Viet Cong encampments. Viet Cong pungee pit trap and two examples of swinging spiked traps.

Figure 63 Laying low during a nearby airstrike, flying in a helicopter, interacting with local children.

Then, we had to survive the helicopter rides; they were an easy target for the Viet Cong to shoot down. Unfortunately, I saw many of my fellow brothers shot down. If we survived all of that, we still had a constant fear of rocket attacks, which were very common.

Figure 64 It seemed like we were on the choppers at least 2 - 3 times a week, going in and out of the rice paddies or jungles. This was my life.

Figure 65 Various munitions - rifle rounds and explosives

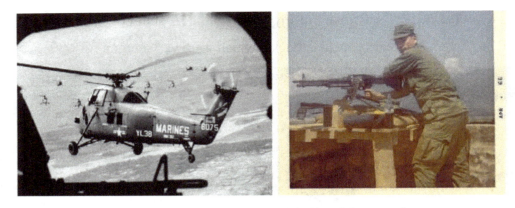

Figure 66 Helicopter sortie, M60 7.62 caliber machine gun

Figure 67 M60 7.62 caliber machine gun and shoulder-fired Rocket-Propelled Grenade (RPG)

Figure 68 .50 caliber machine gun nest, mortar, and local wildlife

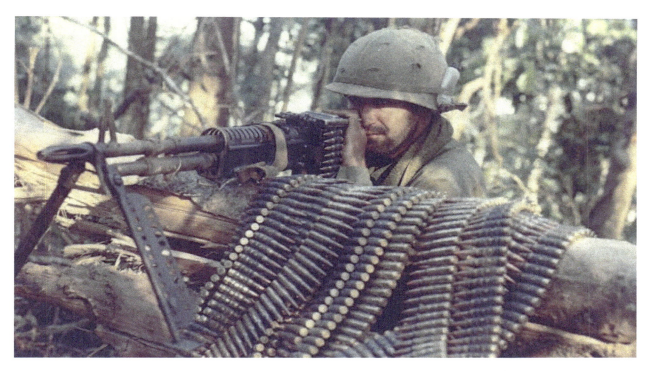

Figure 69 In 1966, my buddy with an M1966-60 machine gun, doing his thing!

Figure 70 Vietnamese girl with a dropped U.S. Bomb that did not go off

However, what worried us Marines the most was the snipers. I remember being out on patrol one day when our lead man took a bullet through his helmet, which killed him instantly (God bless my friend). I can also recall 1966, "Operation Utah," where the 4th Marines were under severe attack from a nearby hillside. We were choppered in to help them out, and as we got closer to the ground, I could see body bags and dead Marines everywhere. I helped to load the helicopters with body bags.

Figure 71 Year 1966 – Operation Utah and Chu Lai - As you can see in the picture, two bullets hit my gun belt. One went through my canteen, and the other grazed my magazine, just missing the primer.

I will never forget the napalm that was dropped on the hill near us, which scorched the entire hillside and everything on it. I remember that we went up the hillside later and saw bodies that were burned beyond belief, as well as a Viet Cong anti-aircraft gun with part of the barrel melted down. My goal was to survive and return to my family and, of course, the ladies. However, most guys received "Dear John" letters when their girls back home broke up with them.

Figure 72 Napalm airstrike. It seemed like this was an everyday type thing!

Unfortunately, I had a minor run-in with a thunderous explosion and had to get 23 stitches in my chest. I later received a purple heart. I believe that it was from our own big artillery, which rained down on us by mistake. I believe that I had courage, even under the toughest circumstances when I was scared to death. In order to keep myself going, I dreamt of returning home.

Figure 73 Some of the weapons we captured

Figure 74 Riding on a tank in a sandbag nest

I really sympathized with the local civilians in Vietnam, living in areas where we were fighting. Many of them had nothing to do with the war and had nothing more than their rice paddies and straw shacks. I always went out of my way to help them in any way that I could.

Figure 75 Some of the kids from the local villages

Figure 76 It seems that the village kids were always after me because I always gave them candy bars and whatever I could.

Figure 77 Year 1966 – Da Nang, Vietnam

Tragically, too many of them were in the wrong place at the wrong time and paid the ultimate price.

I always believed that we did the best we could possibly do, but unfortunately for all of us there, the politicians and the anti-war protestors screwed everything up. I believe that Jane Fonda (the traitor bitch) did more damage to our troops and their morale than she will ever realize. She should have been tried for treason.

Figure 78 Vietnamese currency

It has been more than 55 years for me, and I am finally putting something into words. I took most of the pictures shown in this book, but I chose to leave out most of the pictures showing dead bodies (both Marines and Viet Cong), as they bring nothing but bad memories. I took these pictures and sent the rolls of negatives to my mom (who developed the pictures for me).

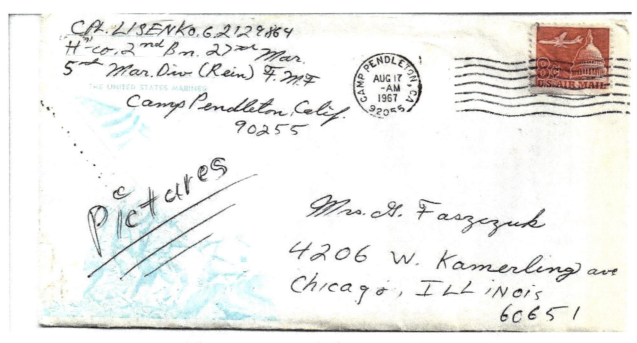

Figure 79 I didn't see the pictures I sent home until years later. I took over 300 pictures; the more I was told not to take pictures, the more I took, to let the pictures do the talking for me.

NOTE – By the way, when I left Vietnam, we were not losing the war!!!

LCPL George LISENKO / 2129864

Combat History Expeditions
1st Battalion, "Alfa" Company, 3rd Marines
Fleet Marine Force, Pacif**

Partcipated in Operations against Viet Cong forces at DANANG RVN from 18Nov65 to 22Jan66.

	From	To
Participated in Operation MALLARD, Quan Nam Province RVN	11Jan66	17Jan66
Participated in Operation Long Lance, DANANG RVN	18Jan66	23Jan66

Combat History Expeditions
1st Battalion, "Bravo" Company, 7th Marines
Fleet Marine Forde, Pacific

Partcipated in Operations against Viet Cong forces at CHU LAI RVN from 24Jan66 to 10Oct66.

	From	To
Participated in Operation UTAH, Quang Ngai Province, RVN	5Mar66	9Mar66
Participated in Operation INDIANA Quang Ngai Province RVN	27Mar66	30Mar66
Participated in Operation NEVADA Quang Nagi Province, RVN	12Apr66	17Apr66
Partiśipated in Operation MONTGOMERY Quang Ngai Province, RVN	9May66	14May66
Participated in Operation MOBILE Quang Ngai Province RVN	25May66	29May66
Participated in Operation FRANKLIN Quang Ngai Province RVN	25Jul66	29Jul66
Participated in Operation JACKSON Quang Ngai Province RVN	27Aug66	30Aug66
Participated in Operation FRESNO RVN	9Sep66	16Sep66
Participated in Operation GOLDEN FLEECE RVN	17Sep66	27Sep66

Rotated to CONUS on 10 October 1966, to 5th Marine Division, Camp Pendleton, California.

George Lisenko
(Signature)

Bruce J. Angelini
Commanding Officer

Figure 80 George Lisenko's Combat History

Additional Pictures for the Vietnam Era

Figure 81 George Lisenko, USMC.

Figure 82 Villagers using elephants

Some villagers in the high mountains in Vietnam used elephants to move around with. The V.C. also used elephants to move heavy arms. I, for one, felt sorry for the villagers as they had nothing to do with the war, and I'm sure they had no idea why we were there!

Figure 83 George Lisenko, his bullet-proof canteen, and a Vietnamese villager.

Figure 84 Newspaper clippings about the Vietnam War.

How to Succeed With an 8th Grade Education by: George Lisenko

Figure 85 Troop transports, investigating a Viet Cong tunnel, local villagers, and a rice paddy.

Figure 86 Marching

Figure 87 Riding on Armored Personnel Carriers (APCs)

Figure 88 Group prayer while deployed

Figure 89 Vietnamese currency, church service on deployment, and Chinook helicopters

Figure 90 Medical helicopter transport, Vietnamese town, a destroyed home, and a rat found in the bivouac

Figure 91 U.S. infantry transportation and Vietnamese transportation

Figure 92 U.S. troops awaiting the arrival of helicopters

Figure 93 This is a monument in Washington, D.C. – A must-see!

I'm Coming Home

I did my part in the hell-hole called 'Nam, then returned back to the world. I landed in Okinawa, and from there, I flew to El Toro Air Base in California. I landed at 3:00 AM and then took a cab to LAX in Los Angeles, CA. The first thing I did was change into civilian clothes. I then took another flight out of LAX and landed at O'Hare airport in Chicago, IL, where I got into a cab and went home. Mom had no clue that I was home on leave, and, of course, she was happy to see me; I was happy to be home. Victor was proud of me and took me to his favorite Ukrainian bar, treating me as his son. From that point on, we respected each other and had a great relationship for the rest of his time on this earth. I was able to catch up with my friends. And, just like that, it was time to go back to California.

I started spending time in Lynwood, CA, on the weekends with my then-best friend John (I called him E.J.). It wasn't long before I met Pat, so I started spending time with her. Then, I ran into Lelah Fisher, and one could say that I fell for her. She was 17 years old, good-looking, tall at 5'11" with long legs and a dark tan on 95% of her body (the other 5% were jet white!). She lived with her brother, Mickey, and a girl named Debbie. Before I knew it, Lelah was pregnant. I didn't know what to do, but I just couldn't leave her, especially after what my father did to my mother and what I did to Barbara. At the time, I liked her a lot, but I couldn't say that I loved her. However, as time passed, I fell in love with her.

I remember that as time drew closer to my discharge, I was told by my lieutenant that we had a parade coming up on the weekend. I requested that I not attend, as my girlfriend Lelah was pregnant and not feeling well, and she and I would be married soon. My request was denied, so my friend Danny and I decided to go U.A. (unauthorized absence). We returned to our station on Monday and were charged with desertion. Danny said that he couldn't care less, but I didn't see it that way. We both got busted, we had one rank taken away, lost money, and we were both charged with a "short-timer's attitude." I decided to see a Navy lawyer, and that is when shit hit the fan. I was called into my captain's office, and he had a fit and said, "What the FUCK is going on with this Navy lawyer?" I said, "Sir, my wife-to-be Lelah is pregnant and is very sick in the hospital, and I asked permission to go to see her rather than to go to a parade, and I was told no." To make a long story short, my captain told me to contact my lawyer and to tell him that I had changed my mind. My captain dropped all of the charges, reinstated my rank, gave me my money back, and offered me the rank of Sergeant if I reenlisted. I was also offered $2,000, which would buy me a new 1967 Chevy Super Sport. However, because of Lelah, I had to say, "Thanks, but no thanks," and I was discharged in December of 1967.

Back to Civilian Life (Marriage to Lelah)

Eventually, I called my mother and told her that I would not be returning to Chicago; and I added, "I met a girl, and I am going to get married, and that's that." Lelah and her mother, Rosemary, made plans for us to get married in Las Vegas. I can clearly remember Lelah asking me, "Well, aren't you going to ask me to marry you?" I replied, "Well, we are on the way to Vegas to get married, aren't we?" I don't think that is what she wanted to hear.

Lelah Ann Fisher and I got married on December 9, 1967.

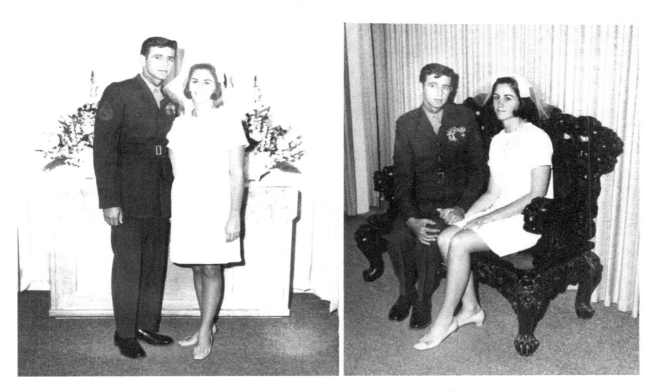

Figure 94 Year 1967 – George Lisenko & Lelah Ann Fisher (wedding pictures)

I started working as a machinist for $1.55 an hour, with an overnight differential of $0.10 an hour additional (which I did since we needed the money). We moved into an apartment in Lynnwood, CA. I didn't have a car, so I had to walk to work and back home (as they say, one has to crawl before one can walk). We saved up $500, and my brother-in-law, who worked at a car lot, helped us get a 1964 Pontiac Bonneville.

Figure 95 Year 1964 - Pontiac Bonneville

Raising Kids

My beautiful Lynne Marie was born on June 19, 1968, coming into the world weighing 9 pounds and 13 ounces and measuring 21 inches long.

Figure 96 Year 1968 – Top left: Lelah 3 months pregnant. Top right: Lelah carrying Lynne. Bottom left: Lynn Marie (my daughter). Bottom right: Lynne with my mom.

Soon after Lynn was born, Lelah got a job as a secretary. We were both very happy at the time. I clearly remember sending my father a short note with a picture of me in my Marine Corps uniform. Sadly, there was no reply. I am not sure whether he received the note or if his wife, Rosemary, received the note and never showed it to him.

Figure 97 George, Lelah, and Lynn

In the year of 1969, Lelah's mother (Rose) and her husband (Jerry) weren't getting along well for whatever reason. Jerry bought a new 1969 Plymouth GTX 440, and I fell in love with the car. It wasn't long before Jerry just got up and split. Unfortunately, Rose couldn't afford the payments, so Lelah and I took the car.

Figure 98 Year 1969 – Plymouth GTX 440

My sister, Olga, came out to visit that year. I told her to take the car around the block, and she did. However, it seems that she managed to hit a parked car. It was no big deal in those days; I gave the guy a few bucks, and that was that. Not long after, we traded the GTX in for a Dodge Charger big block 440.

Figure 99 Dodge Charger big block 440

The Charger was a nice ride; unfortunately, it leaked, and I remember the floor mats were soaking wet. We took it in twice to get it fixed, but it still leaked. The third time we took it in, we ended up trading it in for a 1971 Dodge Challenger big block.

One night after Lelah got off of work. She asked me to meet her at a bar for a drink with some of her coworkers. I found a babysitter for Lynn and met Lelah at the bar. As I walked in, I saw Lelah and another girl sitting with some 6 or 7 guys, and that just didn't feel right to me, so I told her that I thought we should leave. She got up and got into her car, and I got into my truck. She got on the freeway, and she was driving so fast that there was no way that I could keep up with her, so that was the last I saw of her that evening. I went home and received a call from Lelah around 1:00 AM or so. She told me that she got into a car accident but was ok. Somehow, she managed to get a ride home. The next morning, I called her brother, Mickey, and we drove out to the scene of the accident. It was easy to find since some bushes and a tree that she ran into were knocked down. We drove to the nearest junk yard, and we found her Dodge. It was totaled. I am not sure, to this day, whether she was drunk or fell asleep at the wheel.

Back in that time, I was really interested in dune buggies. I had a 2-seater single-rail and also a 4-seater. I had lots of fun going out to Glamis Dunes, Pismo Beach, and Dumont Dunes! I even used to build them in my garage. My Lynne used to say, "Daddy, don't go too fast!" I took my sand-rail and my 4-seater to the L.A. Custom Car and Hot Rod show. I took 1st place in both categories.

At one point, I wanted Lelah to drive the 2-seater, so she got behind the wheel. She was not used to driving a stick shift but did pretty well for a while until she had to stop for a small cliff. Instead of hitting the brakes to stop, she accidentally hit the gas and went over a cliff nose-first.

This bent up the front end, and we both hurt our backs. The pain from the crash bothered Lelah and I for years to come.

Figure 100 Figure 81 Dodge Challenger after Lelah drove it off a cliff.

Figure 101 Picture of Mickey and his wife, Debbie, as well as Danny and his wife. Both of them had dune buggies.

Figure 102 Records from 1966 – 1969

    The year 1969 was the year of the hippies. I had no use for any of them and 0 respect for the lazy, dirty-ass, pot-smoking hippies who seemed to only want sex, weed, and free things. Most of all of them were anti-war and wanted to protest just for something to do. They just weren't all there!

How to Succeed With an 8th Grade Education   by: George Lisenko

Figure 103 Year 1969 – Woodstock and hippies

Figure 104 Records from the early 1970s.

Records from 1970 – "Hitchin' a Ride" by Vanity Fare, "Love Grows Where Rosemary Goes" by Edison Lighthouse. Records from 1971 – "She's a Lady" by Tom Jones, "Joy to the World" by Three Dog Night. Records from 1972 – "Brandy" by Looking Glass. Records from 1973 – "Don't Rock the Boat" by The Hues Corporation, "Come and Get Your Love" by Redbone, "Could it be I'm Falling in Love" by The Spinners. Records from 1974 – "Rock Your Baby" by George McCrae

In 1970, my mom called me and said, "I want to buy a house in California for the future, so you guys start looking for a house, and I'll make the down payment on it." Lelah and I started looking for houses in Norwalk, CA, since Lelah's brother, Mickey, and his wife, Debbie, had just bought a house in that area. Not too long after beginning our search, we found a house for $22,000, and my mom gave us around $500 to put towards the down payment. Our payments were approximately $190 a month, and mom paid for half of the mortgage payments for a year or so. I told Lelah, "Look, my mom doesn't want the house. She just wanted us to have a house, and we need to make the payments ourselves." After that, Lelah and I assumed the whole mortgage ourselves. I was very grateful to my mom for what she did for us to have a house, and maybe that is one of the reasons I did all that I could for my mom over the coming years.

Figure 105 My beautiful mother, Galina. I miss her more and more with each day that goes by. I can't help but tear up when I look at her pictures. To me, she was the best mother one could ask for. She was very talented and could do almost anything.

Figure 106 George and his accidental owl

One day in the summer of 1972, me and my next-door neighbor, Larry, decided to take some of our guns out and go shooting after work. So, we loaded up and headed to Corona (not populated at that time), only some 20 minutes from the 91 freeway. While shooting at targets, I got out my 12 gauge shotgun and shot up a large tree just for the fun of it. All of a sudden, a large OWL came falling out of the tree. It looked like I wounded it. I tried to pick it up, and it bit me, so I got a pair of gloves and wrapped the owl in a towel, and took it home. Went out and got a cage for it and slowly got it back to health by feeding it mice from the local pet store. After a few months, the owl and I became friends, and it looked to me like the owl (I called him Harry) had recovered 100%. So, one day I took Harry back to the same tree and released him right under the same tree, he took a few steps, looked at me, and flew up the same tree, and that was that I still think of Harry the owl every here and there!

Figure 107 My Dune Boggy days with the Over the Hill Gang (picture taken in early '70s in Glamis Sand Dunes

Figure 108 My Mom, Step Dad at Olgas Wedding Day

    1972 was a good year. Lelah and I were getting along pretty well. However, she started to go out with her coworkers after work, and that didn't sit well with me. I guess I was the jealous type. Maybe I should have been, or maybe I should hot have been; I guess we will never know. Lelah was a very good mom; She loved Lynne and took good care of her. She was not the greatest cook, but she made outstanding desserts as well as the best cakes.

    In 1973, Lelah and I started having some issues. She said that I was hard to get along with. Maybe I was hard to get along with because I was too jealous, and I worked 12 hours a day. We had a good love life and were able to make up and move on.

    1974 was not the best year, as Lelah and I encountered more marital problems. I was very much in love with her, and I did my best to keep us together. Unfortunately, sometimes your best isn't good enough, and Lelah ended up moving out. She got an apartment in the same building as her mother, Rosemary. After 2 or 3 weeks, Lelah and I were able to reconcile, and she decided to come back home to me. She said, "I know that you have always wanted a boy." That was music to my ears. So, just like that, Lelah became pregnant with our second child.

Lenny James was born on May 17, 1975. I remember asking the nurse in the lobby, "Is it a boy or a girl?" She replied with, "You'll have to ask your wife." I asked, "Can you just tell me if the baby weighed more or less than 10 pounds?" She replied that the baby weighed more than 10 pounds. I exclaimed, "Wow, that must be a boy!" So, that was great, and I was one happy guy!

Back to Single Life (Divorce from Lelah)

Everything between Lelah and I was fine for a while. However, Lelah and I finally broke up for good in 1976. I felt lost, as I did not want any part of the breakup. I still loved Lelah and wanted her back, but it just wasn't meant to be. I remember going back to my house and finding some guy in the kitchen; that really hurt me. A few weeks later, I was out with a girl named Susie, and as I turned around, I saw that Lelah was right next to me. That evening, Lelah called me and said, "That really hurt me." I replied with, "So now you know what it feels like." My family really loved Lelah and were devastated when they found out about our breakup. But, as we all know, life must go on one way or another. As time passed, Lelah's mother convinced Lelah to consult with a lawyer and to go after me for child support. I asked Lelah not to, but her mother told her, "What if he runs off to Chicago?" That hurt, as I would never run off from my kids; I loved them to death! The bottom line was that I never missed a child support payment. Every Friday, I slipped an envelope under her door. I took the kids every other weekend and never missed my weekends with them.

Figure 109 "We Just Disagree" by Dave Mason - This song reminded me of my Lelah

How to Succeed With an 8th Grade Education													by: George Lisenko

Figure 110 Records from the late 1970s.

Records from 1974 to 1977 – Records from 1974 - "You're the First, the Last, My Everything" by Barry White, "How Long" by Ace, "Get Down Tonight" by K.C. and the Sunshine Band. Records from 1975 - "The Hustle" by Van McCoy. Records from 1976 - "You'll Never Find a Love Like Mine" by Lou Rawls, "Heaven Must Be Missing an Angel" by Tavares, "Disco Inferno" by The Tramps. Records from 1977 – "Shake Your Booty" by K.C. and the Sunshine Band, "Dancing Queen" by Abba. I can remember every one of the songs, who I was with, and what I was doing at the time.

Disco Fever

1978 was a good year for me. I hung out at Disco Techs looking for girls to photograph and just having a good time.

Figure 111 George's photoshoots

Figure 112 George Lisenko during his disco days (c. 1981)

How to Succeed With an 8th Grade Education   by: George Lisenko

Figure 113 My Disco days. I loved to dance; I won some money and some other stuff for first place in dance competitions. Those days were a lot of fun.

Later on, my beautiful daughter Lynne called me one evening and said, "Dad, can you come to pick me up? I want to live with you." I couldn't believe what I was hearing; I simply had no idea what was going on, and I told Lynne, "I'm on my way." When I arrived, Lynne was sitting on the front porch, waiting for me. She got into my car and simply said, "Dad, I don't want to live with Mom anymore!" All I know is that I was not one to say "no" to my kids. I figured that after a few days, whatever it was would blow over, and she would go back to her mother. However, this was not meant to be. It was very sad for me; let's just say that it's a long story, and we will leave it at that. Lelah would call for Lynne, wanting to talk to her, but Lynne just did not want to talk to her mother. I tried my best to have Lynne talk to her mother, but she continued to say, "No." From my point of view, Lelah wanted Lynne to come back, but for me, it was simple: Lynne was old enough to make up her own mind, and she wanted to stay with me. I told Lelah that I would bring Lynne back if Lynne wanted to go back to her, but I would not force Lynne to go back to her. Lynne and I got along great, and I always put her as #1 in my life, but I only had one rule: no boys until she was 16 years old (that was a problem).

In the meantime, Lelah's mother, Rosemary, convinced Lelah to take me to court, so she did. I sent Lynne to my mother's house in Wisconsin for the summer. While Lynne was there, she wrote a note which said, "To whom it may concern: My father did not kidnap me. I want to live with my dad, and I love him very much." I got lucky with the judge, as he awarded full custody to me. I did feel sorry for Lelah, and I remember her asking me to promise not to take Lenny. I simply said, "I did not ask for Lynne, and I will not ask for Lenny, but remember that I love my kids as much as you do and will never say 'no.'"

I continued to date other women, and Lynne never seemed to have a problem with it. As a matter of fact, the girls that I dated loved Lynne, and she was good with that. In the 1980s, I remember taking Lynne to a nightclub with me. She was only 15 years old, but she looked much older, so I put Lynne behind the wheel of my 1977 Pontiac Trans Am.

Figure 114 1977 Pontiac, Trans AM

Ana Fever

In early 1983, my single days came to a stop! One day, on a Thursday night, I got dressed up and hit up Bobby McGee's Night Club. I loved to dress well and smell good. To me, the best-looking and the prettiest ladies hung out at the Disco Techs. As I walked in, I spotted a beautiful woman standing next to two other women. I went to the bar and ordered a beer (I never got into drinking much, perhaps because of Victor and his drinking). I walked up to one of the girls that I spotted, Patty, and asked her about her friend, Ana. For whatever reason, Patty told me that her friend Ana was taken, so I was very disappointed, but I let it go and moved on. However, as luck would have it, I went to the same club a few months later, and I spotted Ana with her mother, Irma. This time, I moved in on Ana and found out that she was not hooked up. It didn't take long before I got Ana's number. I called her the next day and invited her out to dinner. I drove to Ana's apartment, and although I had a bad toothache, I asked her where she wanted to go to eat. Ana said, "How about we stay here, and I will cook dinner here." I was totally impressed, as most girls would rather go out to a restaurant rather than cook, so I knew that there was something special about her. Additionally, Ana's place was spotless!

Ana had just arrived from Peru, and she didn't speak English too well, but I loved her accent. It was just a matter of days before I fell in love with her, but what's not to love? In my eyes, she is simply beautiful and incredibly sexy, she looked better than any girl I was with, and she was by far the best lover a man could ask for. I was truly in love!

Figure 115 My beautiful wife, Ana. What more could a man ask for? She is beautiful, a great dancer, my best friend, and my lover! I have to say: this was the best time of my life.

Ana's mother came out to visit her, so Ana and I spent a lot of time at my place. Not long thereafter, her mother returned to Peru. In the meantime, Lynne was getting into trouble with the boys, and I wasn't having any of it, so she moved back in with her mom. We decided that Ana's place was in a better place than my neighborhood in Long Beach, CA, so I moved in with her. We decided to live on my check alone and to put her money into a bank to save for a house. It wasn't long before we had enough for a down payment for a house, so we found one for $134,000. In the meantime, her roommate, Carina, moved on: it was time. I missed our beautiful roommate, and we wished her the best of luck. I married my best friend, Ana, in Las Vegas on May 12, 1984, with a few friends in attendance. And, just like that, it was time to start a new life with my beautiful Ana by my side.

Figure 116 George and Ana's wedding in Las Vegas on May 12, 1984

Career Advancement

We moved into our house in July of 1984. Ana had her job, and I was working as a manager at a machine shop. I needed a secretary, so I hired Ana, and she quickly caught on to her new role as a secretary at my job. Now, I couldn't ask for anything more. Ana and I were able to be around each other 24 hours a day; we got along great at work as well as at home. On weekends, we traveled to different places in California, like Santa Barbara, San Francisco, Palm Springs, Big Bear, and Hurst Castle. We also traveled outside of California, like Lake Havasu, AZ, and Laughlin, NV. I also took Ana to Chicago, IL, to meet my family, and they simply fell in love with her.

In 1985, Ana traveled to Peru to visit with her family. During Ana's trip, someone broke into her aunt's home and stole Ana's purse with all of her documents in it, which was a serious problem. Ana had a cousin in the military, and he put out the word that there would be a high price to pay if Ana's purse wasn't turned in. Long story short, Ana's purse did show up with everything in it, aside from her money.

Back in 1984 - I took Phil, a business client (purchasing agent), and Diana, his wife, out to dinner. During dinner, Phil said, "George, why don't you open up your own shop?" It's funny that he said that because the thought of opening up my own business had been on my mind for some time. I replied, "I would love to, but it takes a lot of money, which I don't have, and a commitment from someone to give me some purchase orders." Phil stated, "No problem, I will give you enough work." After this conversation, I started thinking more seriously about opening my own business. I didn't really have any money to speak of, but I was a pretty good machinist, I knew a lot of people, and I knew where all of the bodies were buried (meaning that I knew the trade secrets due to my long experience in working with machinery). So, I said to myself, "It's now or never!" and I went for it.

After making the decision to own my own business, one of the first things I did was to pitch my idea to my good friend, Danny. He was also a very good machinist and worked as a salesman with a company in Wisconsin. He didn't have a lot of money, but he had just recently received a $3,000 bonus, and I managed to come up with about $10,000. We named our company: Omni. We went out and purchased a lathe machine and a milling machine. We made a deal to go 50/50 since I needed him, and he needed me. I also made a deal with my friend, Efren, who has a small machine shop. I asked him if I could share his building and rent costs with him. At the time, Efren had 4 machines, and Danny and I had two machines.

I sent Danny to see Phil, and he gave us a purchase order for around $800. It wasn't much, but it was a start. We started to make some money, but it was all put back into the company. Thank God for Ana; she was bringing home more money than me. I knew a lady that worked for a large

Aerospace company as an inspector, and she was able to get us approved to do work for her company. So, next, I sent Danny to Lockheed Aerospace, which was our first large company to work with but not our last.

Figure 117 Lenny's rooftop artwork and some of the machines at Omni.

Soon enough, we had about 12 customers. I started calling DISC (Defense Industrial Supply Center) and giving them a sob story, where I said, "Look, you guys up there owe me a break, I served in the Marines, and I'm a small businessman." It took a while, but one day, I received a call from a guy from DISC. He gave me a number, which turned out to be a facility code number, to do work for the government. That was a big deal, and we started doing a lot of work for them. At one point, we had over 100 customers. Danny quit his job in order to work full-time at Omni. The deal was simple: Danny ran the office, and I ran the shop. Because of my lack of education, I figured that Danny was smarter than me. I was wrong.

Figure 118 Year 2005 (approx.) - Some of Lenny's artistry on the 12,000 square foot Omni building, photographed by a helicopter flying above the building.

Some of my son's handiwork. Sometimes, when he got bored after work, he would get up onto the roof of our building and create art. It took him approximately 4 months and over 100 spray cans to create this scene on our 12,000-square-foot building. When Lenny was finished with this scene, he hired a helicopter to fly over the building and take this picture. The funny thing is that I didn't find out about the artwork until around 6 months later. When I asked him why he did this, he simply said, "It was something to do!" He also said that our building was in the direct flight path for the LAX Airport, so the planes flew directly over the building. How cool is that?! And, sure enough, the next time I flew over our building from LAX, there it was.

1984 was a very busy year for us.

The Father of All Calls

Sometime in late 1985, I was in my backyard cleaning our pool when Ana called out, "You have a phone call!" It turned out to be my dad, Albert. I wondered to myself, "Why, now, after all of these years?" After getting on the phone with Al, he told me, "You know your mother is suing me." I was in total shock and replied, "What? I have no idea what you are talking about. Let me call you back." I immediately called my mom and said, "What the hell is going on with my dad?" Mom started to cry, stating, "He never did anything for you, and now that you have opened your own business, he should help you." I told my mom, "You know I love you more than anything in this world, but if you don't drop this lawsuit, I will never talk to you again." I called Al back and told him, "You will never hear from her lawyer again." I am sure that he was relieved to hear that.

Al and I talked on the phone for a while, and I told him, "I don't want anything from you; I am doing just fine. However, I would like to meet you someday before you or I cross over to the other side." I told him that I travel to Philadelphia, PA, on business here and there. He told me that he would love to meet me. In the meantime, he started sending me money. I remember telling him, "Please don't send me any more money. I don't need it, and I don't want it, but Mom could have used it back in Germany." Looking back, I should not have said the last part.

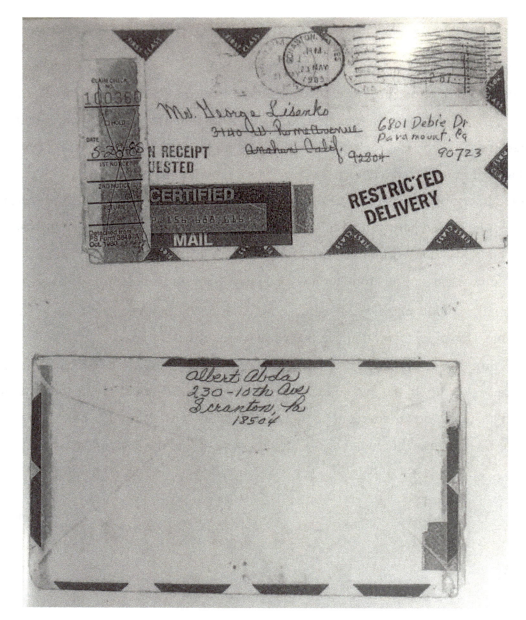
Figure 119 Year 1985 - Letter from Albert Abda (1 of 2)

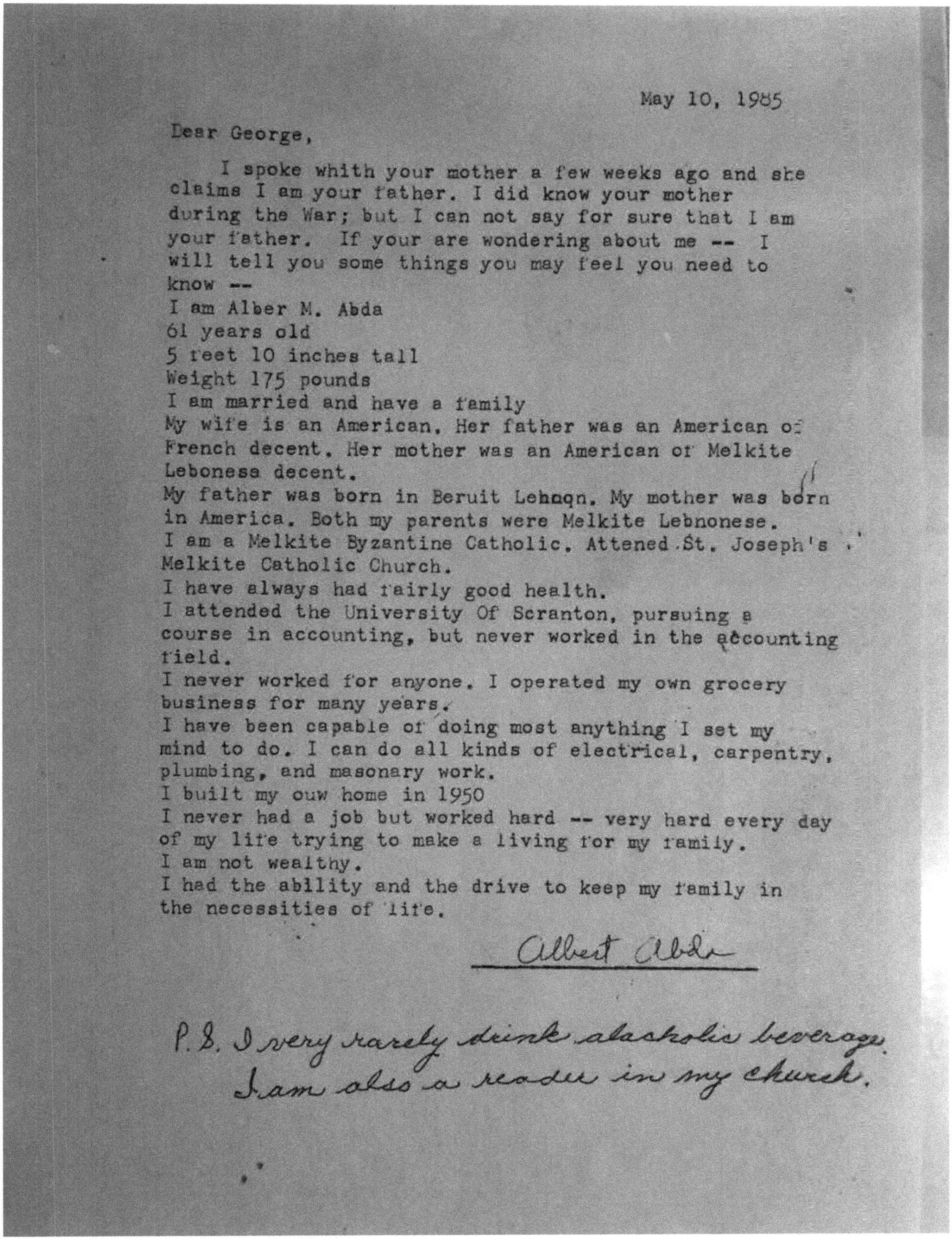

May 10, 1985

Dear George,

I spoke whith your mother a few weeks ago and she claims I am your father. I did know your mother during the War; but I can not say for sure that I am your father. If your are wondering about me -- I will tell you some things you may feel you need to know --
I am Alber M. Abda
61 years old
5 feet 10 inches tall
Weight 175 pounds
I am married and have a family
My wife is an American. Her father was an American of French decent. Her mother was an American of Melkite Lebonesa decent.
My father was born in Beruit Lehnqn. My mother was born in America. Both my parents were Melkite Lebnonese.
I am a Melkite Byzantine Catholic. Attened St. Joseph's Melkite Catholic Church.
I have always had fairly good health.
I attended the University Of Scranton, pursuing a course in accounting, but never worked in the accounting field.
I never worked for anyone. I operated my own grocery business for many years.
I have been capable of doing most anything I set my mind to do. I can do all kinds of electrical, carpentry, plumbing, and masonary work.
I built my ouw home in 1950
I never had a job but worked hard -- very hard every day of my life trying to make a living for my family.
I am not wealthy.
I had the ability and the drive to keep my family in the necessities of life.

Albert Abda

P.S. I very rarely drink alcoholic beverage. I am also a reader in my church.

Figure 120 Year 1985 - Letter from Albert Abda (2 of 2)

Al told me that if I wanted to talk to him for any reason, to reach him at Uncle Johnny's house on Tuesdays. It seems that all 5 brothers met there every Tuesday since they all lived in Scranton, PA. I had the feeling that Al didn't want his wife, Rosemarie, to know that he had reached out to me. I thought to myself, "If I can't call Al at his house, then I just won't call him at all." It was a matter of pride for me, and so it was up to him to contact me. He never did call me back.

Also, in 1985, Ana gave me the big surprise that we were expecting a baby. Alexandra Marie was born on May 15, 1986. She was a shy baby who had a hard time going to preschool, so I had to sneak out when she wasn't looking.

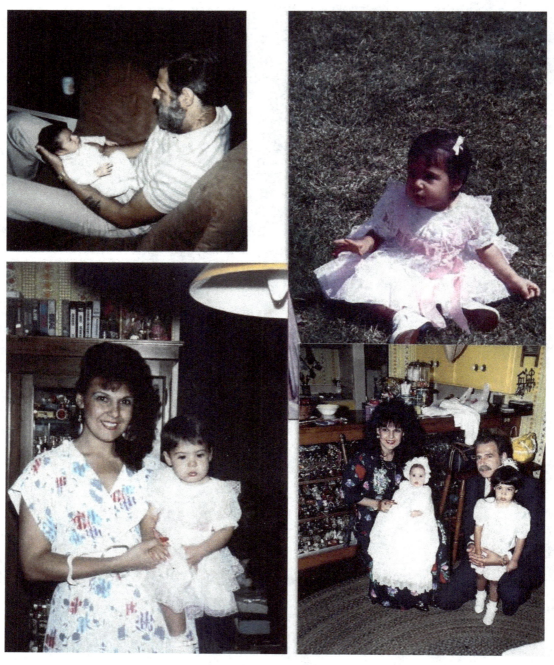

Figure 121 George, Ana, and Alexandra Marie

Figure 122 Year 1990 - Alex at 5 years old

Sometime in 1986, I received a phone call from a man who said, "My mom wants to talk to you." A woman got on the phone and said, "I just wanted to tell you, your father Albert died." Once again, I was in total shock. As it turned out, the man was my Uncle Will, and the woman was his mother, Diamond. Now, I knew why Al never called me back.

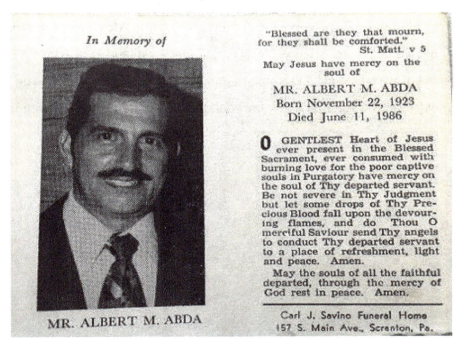

Figure 123 Year 1986 - Obituary for Albert Abda

With enough time lost, I asked Uncle Will about Al's family. He told me that I had 2 sisters, Alexis and Denise, and he gave me their phone numbers. I also remember Uncle Will telling me, "If anyone asks how you got these phone numbers, tell them that Granny gave them to you." Once again, I had the feeling that they were afraid of Al's wife, Rosemarie. From what I understood about her, she was a very good woman, as well as a good mother to her daughters. I believe that she was just trying to protect her girls.

So, now that I had both of my sisters' phone numbers, I asked my wife, "Who do I call first? Alexis, is that she is the eldest or Denise?" Ana advised that I call Denise first. However, I thought that the right thing to do would be to call Alexis, since she is the older sister, so I did. Alexis picked up the phone, and I said, "Your father is also my father." I am sure that she had no idea what I was telling her. She said, "If you are trying to tell me that my father, whom I love and respect, wouldn't tell me this, I just don't believe it." I replied, "How do you think I felt all of these years? Anyways, ask your mother if you have a brother, and she will answer 'yes' or 'no.'" Alexis replied, "My mom is in the hospital, but I will ask her." Before ending the call, I told Alexis, "You will not hear from me anymore. It's up to you to call me if you want." I called Denise, and I told her the same information that I told Alexis. However, the conversations went totally different as Denise said, "I have no idea what is going on, but I believe you." Once again, just as I had told Alexis, I told Denise, "I won't be calling back, so it's up to you guys to reach out to me."

It seems that all of Al's brothers knew that he had more kids, but none of Al's kids knew anything about me. It wasn't long before Alexis called me back, where she said, "I asked Mom about you, and she said 'yes'." I figured that enough time had been wasted where I hadn't met my other siblings from my father. Denise lived in Albany, NY, while Alexis lived in Philadelphia, PA. I told Ana, "Get us two tickets to Albany, New York." Once we landed in Albany, NY, my sisters met us at the airport. It was the end of December, and it was freezing cold. It was around 0 degrees F outside, which was a shock for Ana since she was from Peru and had never been in cold weather before.

Figure 124 Year 1986 (late December) – I love this picture with my two beautiful sisters. Left: Denise? Middle: Me. Right: Alexis

Figure 125 George, Niki, Irma, Ana, and Alexis

In 1986, two days before Alex was born, Irma, Ana's mom, came from Peru to stay with us permanently. It worked out very well for Ana and I, for we never had to worry about a babysitter, and we were able to go whenever we wanted to go. In 1989 Niki was born, and it was a blessing to have Irma watch over our two girls. Since having grandma with us, we just managed to travel the world.

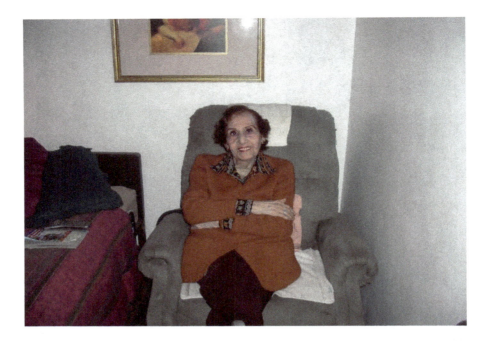

Figure 126 Irma

Figure 127 Alexis, Irma, and Niki celebrating Irma's 101st birthday

Figure 128 Irma celebrating her 106th birthday

Irma was born August 2, 1914, and passed away December 2, 2020, at 106 years old. When you think about it, Irma lived through WWI, WWII, the Korean War, The Vietnam War. The Iraqi War, as well as the Afghanistan War. God Bless her soul and rest in peace. I'm sure she is in a very special place in heaven. Love you, Irma!

...and the Horse You Rode in Place on

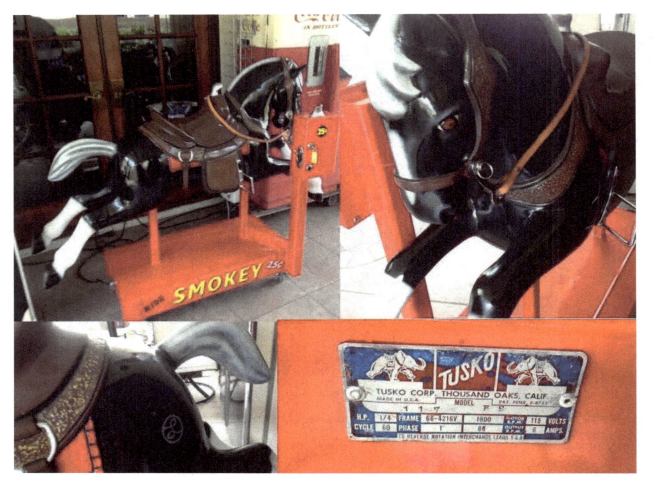

Figure 129 George's questionably-acquired Kentucky Derby thoroughbred, Smokey.

In 1986, I started to look around to buy a horse for my Alex. Back in that time, we didn't have the internet to use to look for one, so we had to go around ourselves to different shops. After a month or so of searching, I gave up. Then, one day, Ana and I stopped at a doughnut shop in a small shopping section around midnight, and as I looked around, there was this horse next to a market. As I walked up to it, I noticed that it was just plugged into the wall. I told Ana, "Let's go home." Then, I got my truck, called one of my friends to come help me, and we both went back to get the horse. We simply picked the horse up and loaded it into my truck, and off we went. We got home and put it in my backyard. When I woke up the next morning, I opened the coin mechanism, and I could hardly believe my eyes: quarters came pouring out! I couldn't care less about the money; I was just happy that my Alex got her horse. I ended up restoring the horse back to mint condition and naming him 'Smokey'. The funny thing is that one of my good friends from some 15 years ago, who was younger than me by 20 years, saw the horse and said, "Hey, I used to ride one that looked just like this one." As it turns out, the same horse he used to ride when he was a kid was stationed at the same spot that I swiped Smokey from.

In 1987, my cousin, Richard, came out for a visit. He was the first of my cousins that I met. A few years later, my Uncle Joe, the oldest of my dad's brothers, came for a visit. The year after, my Uncle Will and his wife came out for a visit. At the time, the shop was doing pretty well, but we got into trouble with the IRS. We didn't have worker's compensation or healthcare for employees because we were putting every penny earned back into the business. We were able to pay up and move on from that issue.

In 1988, Omni was doing pretty well. I hired Carina, who knew Ana in Peru and was our roommate for 2 years.

Figure 130 Carina with her dog, Strider

I sent her to see Dave often, who was the manager of All Power – a machine shop that made aerospace parts. She picked up parts for us to machine, and also delivered parts back to All Power, so she got to know Dave. We had a party at our house to celebrate Ana's mom's 90th birthday, and Dave and Carina started dating around then and have been together ever since.

Figure 131 Carina and David Mosier

Dave and I have a lot in common and have been friends for many decades. Dave has a machine shop, and I had a machine shop until I sold mine to my son for $1. Dave made money, and I made money. Dave lost lots of money, and so did I. Dave had come from Detroit, MI, and I had come from Chicago, IL. Dave got into trouble with his company, S&S Precision, and I got into trouble with my company, Omni, and we both pulled out of it. The main thing is that Dave has a set of balls on him. When things go bad, you don't give up; you simply stand tall until you get back on your feet again. THAT is my kind of guy, and I would like to think of myself as that kind of guy, too. Overall, we both made our millions. The real question is: Where did it go? That is what the wives want to know!

Niki and the Last of the USSR

In 1988, we received great news again: Ana was pregnant with our second child! Nicole Ana was born on March 3, 1989.

Figure 132 Nicole Ana, through the years.

She was a breach baby, and I remember that Ana and I were so happy with our beautiful girls. At this time, we had been approved to do work for Douglas Aircraft as well as Boeing Aircraft Co., so we were doing very well.

I ended up calling my mom and asking her, "Mom, if you could go to one place in the world, where would you want to go?" She answered, "Russia," without any hesitation. I told Mom, "I'll have Ana make plans." Back in 1989, Russia was still a Communist country, so it would not be easy for U.S. citizens to travel there. It took a while, but eventually, Ana put the whole trip together, tickets and all. Mom flew from her home in Chicago, IL, to California in order to spend a few days with us before our flight to Russia. The night before our big trip, everything was fine, and I remember telling my mom, "Good night, Mom, see you in the morning." On the day of the trip, I went to work for a few hours in the morning since the flight left later in the day. Ana called me at work and told me, "You had better come home now. Your mom is very sick." I rushed home, and by the time I got home, Mom was already in the hospital. Sure enough, she was not responding. There was a lot on the line: my mother, the trip that took forever to put together, etc. I just didn't know what to do. I made the decision to take her out; we were going to Russia, no matter what. The Doctor said, "This lady is not going anywhere." I told my wife, "Honey, put Mom's clothes on. We are leaving." The Doctor said, "There is no way." I replied, "Watch me," as I rolled her out of the hospital and into my car. I knew that if anything happened to Mom, my brother and sisters would never forgive me. I was not sure what was wrong with Mom, but I just figured that it was an anxiety attack, and she could sleep on the plane on the way to Germany as it was a long flight.

By the time we arrived in Germany, Mom was just fine, thank God. We changed planes and headed to Russia, where we had our travel guide, Nadia, waiting for us. We met Victor's sister at our hotel; she and her daughter had traveled by train to meet us in Moscow, Russia. The country was very poor, and so was she. We left one suitcase with her, I believe, and I remember giving her two $100 bills. I can't recall, but I believe that the exchange was somewhere around 15 to 1. I had over $10,000 in a case with me, which I was supposed to declare at the airport, but I didn't.

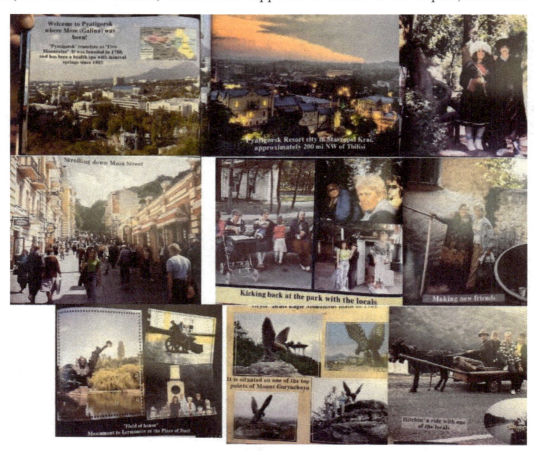

Figure 133 Year 1989 – Trip to Russia – Photo collage

We flew out to my mom's hometown of Pyatigorsk, Mt. Elbrus, which translates to 'Five Mountains and is the highest summit in Europe. The city was founded in 1780 and has been a health spa with mineral springs since 1803.

Figure 134 Year 1989 – Trip to Russia – Mount Goryachaya, Pyatigorsk, Russia – The Eagle Monument - The Brass Eagle had sentimental value to my mother because she and her father took a picture in the same spot as we did, long ago

At one point in the trip, we ended up at a Russian restaurant, where everyone was after my daughter, Lynne, and it also seemed like everyone was very interested in Ana's and Lynne's nails. I told my mom to tell the waitress that I wanted to pay for everyone's meal. I hadn't spent much of the money I brought with me to Russia since I hadn't purchased many items. I paid for everyone's meal in the restaurant, which was less than $50 total.

Figure 135 Year 1989 – Trip to Russia - Every night, we had young guys who would approach our table to talk to Lynne, and to bring flowers to all of the girls

Figure 136 Year 1989 – Trip to Russia - This show was put together specifically for American guests like us

We flew back to Germany, and Mom stayed with one of her friends while Ana and I traveled to Austria, Luxembourg, and several other European countries.

Figure 137 Year 1989 – Trip to Russia – Strolling down Main Street

Figure 138 Year 1989 – Trip to Russia - Ana and I took a picture dressed up in traditional Russian outfits (don't mind the tennis shoes)

Figure 139 Year 1989 – Trip to Russia – Sheep and cows on the road in front of our van

Figure 140 Year 1989 – Trip to Russia – Hitchin' a ride with one of the locals

We then traveled back to Germany, picked Mom up, and flew back to the good old USA.

Figure 141 Traditional Russian dress.

Karen and trip to vegas

Here are pictures of Niki's and Alex's kids

Niki : Karley Ana (8-16-21) and Hailey Nicole (8-7-20)

Alex: Mason Alexander (11-10-21)

George & Barbara (Karen's mom)

In 1990, I decided that it was time to find my daughter, Karen, who we gave up for adoption. It had been many years since 1965, and I had been asking myself how to go about finding her. Well, the first thing I knew I needed to do is to find my old friend, Mike, who I asked to keep an eye on Barbara when I joined the Marines. It took a while, but I was able to track him down, and gave him a call. He told me that the last he knew of Barbara's whereabouts was that she was working in downtown Chicago for Bethlehem Steel Co. So, that was easy enough, and I looked up the company's phone number and made the call. The phone rang, and I heard a woman's voice on the other line say, "This is Barbara, how can I help you?" I replied, "It's been a while. This is George." It took a while, and she just couldn't believe that it was me calling her after all of these years. We talked for a while, and I said to Barbara, "I am looking to find our daughter." She replied, "What? Are you crazy?" I have no idea where she is and how to find her." I told Barbara, "Just give me the name of the hospital that she was born in, and the name of the adoption place that you gave Barbara up to." Barbara told me that she had delivered our child at Grant Hospital, and that our child had gone to Catholic Charities, so that was a start!

Barbara told me that she had married a man named George, who didn't know anything about the baby she previously had. I asked, "Well, where do you stand with this when I find her?" Barbara replied, "First of all, you are not going to find her. But, if you do, then I'll tell my husband and my family about her." I told Barbara, "The next time you hear from me will be when I find her, and I WILL find her."

Now that I had some information, the first thing I did was to call Catholic Charities. I called, and told the person who answered the phone that I was looking for my daughter, and she replied, "Just a minute." Then, another woman got on the phone and said, "This is Kathy, can I help you?" I responded, "Yes, I am looking for my daughter." I gave this woman, Kathy, all of the information that I had, including her birth date of Father's Day 1965. The bottom line was that Kathy said that there was nothing that she could do for me. I was very disappointed, and I couldn't understand why she couldn't help me? I decided that I was not going to take "no" as an answer, so a few days later, I boarded a plane and headed to Chicago. Once I landed, I rented a car and headed to downtown Chicago, got myself a room for the night, and then drove to Catholic Charities the following morning. Once I arrived and entered into the building, I asked for Kathy. She met me in the lobby, and we entered into a private room. Once again, I gave her all of the information that I had. She left the room, and came back with a folder in her hand. I was sure that folder was what I was looking for. However, upon her return to our private room, she asked me, "Why did you give her up?" I said, "Look, Barbara was 15 years old, and I had just joined the Marines. There was no way to take care of the baby. Barbara's mother was a single parent and a waitress being paid minimum wage." Kathy became very rude, and said, "There is nothing I can do for you." I replied, "One FUCKING way or another, even if I have to break in and steal the information, I will find her with or without you." The BITCH, Kathy, said, "For all we know, she could be dead!" So, once again, I was on my own. But one thing was for sure: I was determined to find her.

I started to call different adoption agencies that could help me in my search to find my daughter. The months went by, but one day, I called a company called Adoption Triangle. It was on a Friday afternoon, and I remember the woman I spoke with, Mary Fran, was also looking for her father, so she offered to help people who were searching for their lost parents or children for free. I went to work the next morning, which was a Saturday, and as I walked in, my shop foreman told me that a woman had called looking for me right after I left the office the previous day. I knew it was Mary Fran, and called her back right away. Once I got Mary Fran on the phone, she asked me, "Do you have a pen and paper? Here is your daughter, Karen's, phone number." I replied, "Oh my GOD, thank you so much." I sent Mary Fran 24 red roses and wished her all the best in finding her father.

As it turns out, when Karen was in college, she had to write an article on adoptions, so she also filled out a form with her name, date of birth, and birth hospital, which would be retained if her biological parents were to ever search for her. So, right after Mary Fran and I hung up from our first conversation, she went to her file cabinet, looked back to the year of 1965, verified the date of birth and birth hospital, and there was Karen.

When I first called Karen, I had no idea what to say to her; I just picked up the phone, called her, and said, "Hi, I'm your dad." We had a long talk, and of course, the first thing she asked me was, "What about my mother?" Karen told me that Catholic Charities had called her, and told her, "Your father is looking for you, and we do not recommend a reunification, as he seemed to be on drugs and angry." I have no idea how the CHURCH could say something like that? (By the way, I don't do drugs, and I don't drink very often.) We had a long talk, and she finally got some background information about me.

Later, I called Barbara, and said, "Here is your daughter's phone number. It took some time to find her. The rest is up to you; do what you have to do." As it turns out, Karen and Barbara lived very close to each other, and they both worked blocks apart in downtown Chicago. I wondered to myself how many times they passed each other while walking on the streets?

My family saw Karen two days later, and I sent her two tickets for her and her husband, George, to come out to California. The rest is history! I am not sure why, but it took Barbara almost a week to contact Karen. I guess that Barbara had to take some time to think about what she was going to say. Regardless, Karen was happy to join our family, and we are happy to have her. Karen now lives in Arizona, so we are able to see each other as often as we want. For some reason, sadly, Karen doesn't want much to do with her mother, Barbara.

Goldyn family: Trevor, Monica, George, Karen

In 2003, when our good friend Lili traveled from Chile to California for a visit, we decided to take a trip to Las Vegas, with our friend, Laura, who also joined us. A friend of mine, Dennis, told me that on the way to Vegas, you can take a detour and go through the desert. He said, "Take the turn-off at Afton Road, and it will take you to a beautiful place that looks like the Grand Canyon. So, Dennis drew me a map on a napkin, stating, "It will only be a 20-mile detour, and it will be well worth it at the end. Turn left by the railroad tracks, and it will take you to the town of Baker, and from there, you can get back on the main road and drive to Vegas."

I had just bought myself a brand-new Ford Excursion 4 x 4 with some oversized tires and aluminum mag wheels, so I thought it would be something fun to do. So, we took the turn-off at Afton Rod, and I must say that it was a fun ride with beautiful scenery. We were having a great time and enjoying our trip. I got on one side of the railroad tracks and headed for the road where I could take the turn-off to head to the town of Baker. The next thing I knew, there was a loud noise, and just like that, I had a tire blow out. The right-rear tire swallowed a very sharp, pointed rock, and in a second it was flat. I figured, "No big deal, I'll just change out the tire for my spare." The only problem was that I only had the wrench for the standard tires, and since I had custom ones on, there was no way to change out the tires. So, there we were, stuck in the middle of the desert.

Luckily, two of the girls had cell phones, so I called my daughter, Lynne, at the shop, and I told her to call Dennis and tell him to bring a 15/16 socket and wrench because we were stuck on the left side of the tracks and the phones had no reception," The 2nd cell phone was very low on battery, so I called my daughter and told her to find us. However, before I could finish the phone call, the phone disconnected due to having no reception. Now, there was nothing to do but wait.

We got stuck at around 10:00 am. As the day went on, it became very hot, somewhere around 100 F, and we had no water. I had no idea where we were at, and once the sun started setting, I started thinking about the movie The Hills Have Eyes. Now, it was my job to protect the girls at all costs. As the night went on, trains kept on passing through next to us, so I started flashing my headlights on and off to capture their attention. Now it was midnight, and there was no sign of help. As the night went on, I saw lights off in the distance, and I told the girls that I would walk towards the light at 4:30 am if help hadn't arrived yet. At around 1:00 am, Ana said, "Honey, what's that noise?" I got out of the car, and I could hardly believe it – it was a sprinkler system to keep the brush green so as to keep sand from covering the railroad tracks. Now, if we needed water, all we had to do is break off a sprinkler head. Around 1:30 am, I saw one big light in the distance, which started to slow down miles from us. The single light, which ended up being attached to a train, stopped right in front of us. I was totally impressed! As we looked up at the conductor, I told him, "We got a flat and we are stuck out here." He gave us some cold water and said, "I'll call it in, don't worry, I know exactly where you guys are at." I told him that I was planning on walking towards the lights which were off in the distance, and he said that the lights were coming from the city of Baker, and that it would be a good 60-mile walk. At around 2:00 am, I saw some headlights, and I knew that trains only had one large light. I told the girls to stay in the vehicle and to lock the doors. I found a broken handle from a sledgehammer that was used to drive pins into the railway ties, and I readied myself to use my Marine Corps skills. If something didn't look right, I was ready and willing to shellac whoever it was with my big sledgehammer handle. As the truck got closer, I noticed that it was a beat up, old Chevy pickup truck, somewhere around a 1976 or so. As it stopped near us, I was ready to swing, but then I noticed the t-shirt on one of the two guys which said Afton Road Service. That was a close call.

Anyways, I asked the guy if he had a 15/16 socket, and he handed it to me. I changed the tire myself, and now I had 3 big tires and one small tire, so the truck leaned to one side. I asked the guy, "How much do I owe you?" He said, "I have been looking for you guys for 9 hours, and the bill is $900." At that point, I didn't care, and I gave him the money and we followed him into

Baker. Once we arrived, we got something to eat before getting back on the road and heading to Vegas. I remember when we hit the Hard Rock Hotel, I put a $100 bill into the slot machine, and on the 2nd pull I hit $1,000. I guess one could say that I got my money back.

All-in-all, we had a great time. The lesson here was: Don't pull off the main road into the desert, unless you have someone following you.

Year 2003 - Desert Adventure

Around the World In 80 Months

In the 1990s, we started to travel the world a lot. It seems like every year. We visited at least 3 different countries. So far, I have been to 51 different countries (thanks to Omni), while Ana has been to 41 countries. We are not done with our travels yet, as there is much more out there for us to see, like Lebanon, Egypt, Ukraine, Belarus, Siberia, etc. I have been to Russia 3 times and hope to travel back again. So far, my favorites (in order) are as follows: 1. Russia, 2. Poland, 3. Peru, 4. Spain. I love going places that no one else is interested in, like Mongolia. I have been asked, "Why would you want to go there?" And I reply, "Because no one else wants to!" Here are some pictures of the places that we have visited, which represent just a few of the countries that we have traveled to. In total, I have visited 51 countries, and Ana has visited 45 countries.

Figure 142 Iquitos, Peru

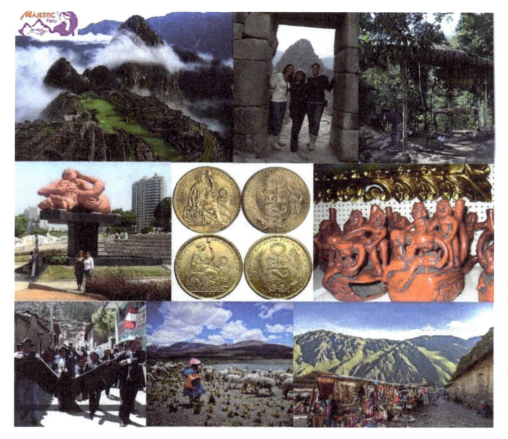

Figure 143 Peru

Figure 144 Lima, Peru

Figure 145 Year 2013 - Budapest, Hungary

Figure 146 Year 2014 – Gothenburg, Norway

Figure 147 Year 2017 - Bucharest, Romania

Figure 148 Madrid, Spain

Figure 149 Year 2015 – Vilnius, Lithuania

Figure 150 Year 2015 - Siauliai, Lithuania - "Land of the Crosses" - The first crosses were erected in 1831 in response to an uprising against Russian rule over the small Baltic country

Figure 151 As we traveled across Europe, we encountered poor beggars in every country. Thank God I was always on the giving end and not the receiving end

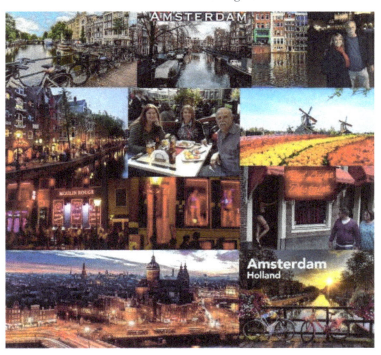

Figure 152 Amsterdam, Netherlands

Figure 153 Chile, South America

Figure 154 Year 2014 – Copenhagen, Denmark

How to Succeed With an 8th Grade Education				by: George Lisenko

Figure 155 Morocco, Africa

Morocco was a totally different world. The center picture was me holding the Alibaba handmade vintage knife. I saw it in a market, and I asked the guy, "How much?" He replied, "$300 because it is very old and rare." I said, "No thanks." He replied, "$250." I said, "No thanks." He replied, "$200." I said, "No thanks." He followed me for two blocks and asked for $150, and I said, "No thanks." He replied, "$100." I said, "No thanks," and we left. Four blocks later, there he was, asking for $50, and I finally said, "Ok." The same thing happened to my wife, and she got some jewelry. I had never seen so many poor kids, so I decided to give my guide $100. And I asked him to get me some change, and he did. I started to hand out the money to the kids, who were between 5-10 years old. Before I knew it, there were more kids after me than I could count. I gave our guide another $100, and once again, he changed it into coins, and I gave it all to the poor kids. The guide asked, "How about me?" I gave him $20 and moved on. On this trip, my wife and kids also got to ride on camels.

Figure 156 Cuba, North America

Cuba was a very poor yet very interesting place to visit. I loved the Cuban people, and I felt like I was back in the 1950s when we were there. It seemed like time stood still since the Americans left when Fidel Castro and his revolution took over in 1959. The government took $20 off every $100 that foreigners exchanged for Cuban currency. The Cuban people are friendly and love the American tourists because Americans hand out pretty good tips. Cuba was off-limits to Americans, so we entered through Mexico. I remember a police officer telling Javier and Patty not to take any pictures, so I took one of him. I would love to go back!

Figure 157 Cuba, North America - Nick and Brody

Figure 158 Cuba, North America - Notice that all of the books are mainly Cuban propaganda from the 50's and early 60's

Figure 159 Year 2012 - Alaska cruise

Figure 160 Year 2012 - Alaska cruise – George & Ana Lisenko

Figure 161 Year 2012 - Alaska cruise - George & Ana Lisenko

Figure 162 Year 2012 - Alaska cruise - Ana, Brenda, Marie, Patty (from left to right)

Travel details by year:

2013: Central Europe: Hungary, Budapest – Vienna, Austria – Czech Republic – Slovakia

2014: Scandinavia – Oslo, Norway – Gothenburg, Sweden – Copenhagen, Denmark

2015: Baltics – Vilnius, Lithuania – Old Riga, Latvia - Tallinn, Estonia – Helsinki, Finland

2016: Russia, Moscow & Old Saint Petersburg

2017: Sofia, Bulgaria – Nis & Belgrade, Serbia – Transylvania & Bucharest, Romania

2019: Costa Cruise: Venice, Italy – Corfu, Greece – Dubrovnik, Croatia

The United States of America v George Lisenko

In late 1999, my nephew, Aaron (my sister, Alexis's son), called me and asked me if I would give him a job. I told him, "Come on out, you've got a job." He came out in September, which was perfect timing because we were moving the shop to a new building in October. Aaron ran the shipping department for years and did a great job. As the years went by, I told Aaron, "You know, you have a great education and a college degree. Why don't you start looking for a better job? I think that you could make a lot more money out there than in here. When you are caught up with your work here and in your free time, go online and look at what's out there on my dime, and if you find something out there, you can set up an interview on my dime as well." He did exactly as I had advised and got himself a great job. He eventually got married and had two boys.

Figure 163 These are some of the parts that we made at Omni.

How to Succeed With an 8th Grade Education
by: George Lisenko

Over 90 percent of them are for the aerospace industry, as well as the government. These are all parts used on the landing gear for commercial planes like: 737, 747, 757, 767, 777, as well as all of the military jets like: F-14, F-15, F-16, F-18 as well as the latest Bombers.

Danny and I started having our differences between 1994 and 1995. It's a very long and complicated story, so I will make it as short as I can. We used to make bushings and bearings as well as other items for the landing gear of airplanes. One day, a lady named Linda Thomson called and said that she was new in this business, and she wanted to know if we had a Douglas blueprint for a part number. I looked it up and told her that we did have that specific blueprint. She wanted to order 2 bushings, so I gave her the price of $500 and made the order; it was no big deal. However, it turned out that she was an FBI agent located in Virginia. Additionally, we didn't know that the part number for this Douglas blueprint was under some licensing agreement and that it was a sole source item to a company in Utah, where we originally received the order from. Unbeknownst to me, we were not allowed to make this part for anyone else.

We received an order for 100 pieces, and then a company called D&D Air also ordered an additional 10 pieces of this specific item. The FBI was after this guy and simply went through our company to get to him. As I said, this became very complicated. The bottom line was that the FBI wanted Danny and I to turn against each other. I didn't buy into that, but Danny did. It seems that D&D Air didn't have an FAA license and forged a stamp.

The FBI asked me if I was aware of the FAA, and I told them that I was not aware of the FAA and had nothing to do with them. All of the companies that we did work for had FAA approvals, and we worked under their umbrellas 100 percent, so it was legitimate. I remember the FBI agent told me, "You know, you're a street-smart guy. You fought in Vietnam, and you built a company once you came home. You must have had a gut feeling that this was wrong, and you are trying to smoke-screen me." For whatever reason, he didn't believe me.

It was a weird feeling to look at my court documents, which read, "The United States of America vs. George Lisenko." Somehow, the FBI got to Danny. When I asked him, "Did you get served?" I couldn't believe it when he replied, "You just have to go to Virginia for yourself." Additionally, he said, "Why did you tell the lady that we were FAA approved?" I replied, "What? I never told her that!" Somehow, the FBI agents had convinced Danny that I did. Sometimes, we just can't trust our own government. Danny was a guy from Chicago, and he and I served in Vietnam together. He was my best man at our wedding, and I was twice his best man at his weddings. He was my business partner, and I wondered to myself, "How could he turn on me?" My wife and Danny's wife, Roxanna, went to school together in Peru. One day, his wife told me, "Danny was scared to death." I told her, "We didn't do anything wrong. God gave us a set of balls, and I am going to use mine. If he can't use his, so be it." Sometimes, when the shit hits the fan, you find out who your friends really are. I can't tell you how disappointed I was in Danny, but I knew one thing: I was not going to cave in. Life must go on, and I had a family to take care of and a company to run.

My plan was to plead "not guilty." I remember what my brother-in-law, who was a lawyer for the state of New York, said to me, "If I was your lawyer, I would win this case as this was clearly entrapment by the FBI. However, if I was the prosecutor, I would simply say, "Ladies and gentlemen of the jury, even though we found the parts to be per blueprint requirements, how would you feel flying 30,000 feet in the air with an unapproved part in your place?" I also remember a Pollack FBI agent telling me, "The jury out here is not like the surfers in California. I got the point, and we got Danny to testify that you knew about the FAA."

I just couldn't get myself to plead guilty to something I knew nothing about. The SCUMBAG of a lawyer who was representing me told me that with my Vietnam record, I would only get a slap on the wrist if I pleaded "guilty." If I pleaded "not guilty" and then lost the trial by jury, I could get 5 years of prison time and a fine. At the last moment, before I entered the courtroom, my wife begged me to plead guilty, so I did. That was one of the hardest decisions I have ever made. In the end, Danny had to serve 8 months, and I had to serve 6 months in an Air Force base emptying waste baskets and cleaning floors. They were easy on us since this was considered to be a "white-collar" crime. Danny and I both served our time, got out, and moved on. Sadly, though, since Danny and I were no longer friends, my wife also lost one of her best friends (Danny's wife).

However, Danny and I still owed the IRS $138,000 from some trouble we got into with them back in 1993. Danny wanted out of the company, so he told me, "If you pay for my share of the money that we owe to the IRS, I will give you my 50% of the company (personally, I thought it was something I could easily live with, but don't tell him that). I told him, "I am not sure who is getting the better deal, you or me, since you will walk out with no debt, and I get stuck with the IRS." I asked my secretary, Moni, to meet me at the shop on Sunday, and we went through the accounting books and found some big mistakes in them. It seemed that Danny plain had his head up his ass. One of Danny's errors was that he wrote a check for $14,000 to a company but never deducted it from the money owed. He made the same mistake with another company, for $3,500. By the time my secretary and I were done fixing Danny's mistakes, we knocked off some $40,000 of what we owed. Now, I could see that I got the better deal by far, but I did not tell him what I found.

Next, I spoke with Rich, who was the IRS agent assigned to my case, and I told him that I would make a payment every Friday until I paid him off. He said, "I have to be honest with you: with companies like yours, there is a 95 percent chance that you won't make it. I told him, "I am in the 5 percent that will make it." He replied, "We will see, but I wish you the best." So, Moni and I went to visit him every Friday, as I had told him I would. We gave him payments of $2,000, then $1,500, then $3,000. One day, he called me into his office and asked me, "How did you get into this position with owing the IRS money?" I told him, "Well, we made an order for Hill Air Force Base for some bushings off of a Lockheed blueprint, and we made it to a 6-dimension, which turned out to be an 8-dimension on clear print. We requested a clear blueprint, and sure enough, it was an 8-dimension, and we got it rejected from the Air Force. I told Rich that my inspector had it as a 6-dimension as well as my operator, and your government inspector bought off on the job. It was worth $38,000, and we had to remake it. Rich asked me if I could prove everything that I had just said, and I answered, "Of course." So, I got him all of the paperwork, and he said, "Wait a minute while I talk to my boss." I waited some 10 minutes, and he came out and told me, "We dropped your debt by $38,000," which got us down to owning $7,000. The following week, Moni and I went to pay him off in full. Sadly, he was transferred back to the main office in Sacramento, CA. I was looking forward to handing him the final payment and asking him, "What was it you said about the 5% that don't make it?" After the IRS was paid in full, Danny signed off on the agreement we made, and it was all on me from then on.

AIR TRANSPORT

BROKERS PLEAD GUILTY TO BOGUS PARTS SALES

JAMES OTT/CINCINNATI

A bogus parts investigation that started at the Defense General Supply Center, Richmond, Va., has resulted in a stiff sentence and large fine for a California parts broker who specialized in landing gear sales.

Two machine shop owners received lesser penalties, and a second California parts broker is awaiting sentencing. The charges are related to falsely documenting replacement parts for U.S. civil and military aircraft, according to the FBI.

The case may spur the U.S. airlines to refile their petition with the FAA calling for an extension of federal regulations to the thousands of unregulated U.S. parts brokers. But since that petition drew strong FAA resistance last year, industry officials are not sure what may result.

INDICTMENTS related to the case were unsealed last week in the U.S. Court for the Eastern District of Virginia at Richmond. Judge James R. Spencer sentenced James L. Daniele, 51, operator of D & D Air, Inc., San Clemente, to a 2.5-year prison term and fined him $250,000. The judge ordered an additional fine derived from the sale of Daniele's seized business property and parts inventory that could total $15 million.

Daniele pleaded guilty to a one-count violation of the Racketeer Influenced and Corrupt Organization (RICO) law. The FBI said Daniele sold $4.2-million worth of unapproved parts between 1990-94. Agents cited wire orders for parts from Airborne Express, World Airways, Cargolux, Continental Airlines and Algonquin, Ill.-based Mitchell Aircraft.

THE FBI said Danny E. Rudd and George Lisenko, each 48 and a partner in Omni Machine Corp., Whittier, Calif., supplied unapproved parts, primarily bushings and bearings, to Daniele. They pleaded guilty to one count of wire fraud each. Rudd was sentenced to seven months' imprisonment, Lisenko to six months, and each was fined $5,000.

A fourth man netted in the investigation, Carlos Del Toro, has pleaded guilty to two counts of wire and mail fraud. U.S. Attorney Helen Fahey said Del Toro fraudulently documented parts through his company, Avion Spares, Inc., and sold them as parts produced under FAA regulations. His sentencing has been scheduled for Mar. 27.

The probe began with the Defense Criminal Investigative Service of the inspector general's office of the Defense Dept., and later included the FBI, the Transportation Dept.'s inspector general and the FAA. It began as early as 1992 in Richmond and then spread to California.

Sarah MacLeod, executive director of the Aeronautical Repair Station Assn., Alexandria, Va., said the government does not enforce compliance with FAA regulations at the site of parts manufacturing.

MD-11 CHECK FOR CRACKS

LOS ANGELES

McDonnell Douglas MD-11 transport operators have been requested by an FAA airworthiness directive to inspect for possible cracks in part of the aircraft's engine pylon box structure.

THE ISSUING of the directive follows the recent discovery of a crack found in an upper spar angle on an American Airlines trijet during a routine inspection. Douglas Aircraft Co. officials said about 90% of the MD-11 fleet had been inspected by mid-week last week, and that only one other pylon crack had been found by that time.

The problem was believed to be the result of a failure to adequately heat-treat the pylon component, which makes the part subject to stress corrosion. A U.S. MD-11 subcontractor provided the part in question for the pylon, for which Rohr is the primary subcontractor. Douglas last week was preparing a service bulletin for the continued inspection of the pylon.

Meanwhile, Douglas is continuing to weigh the possibility of suspending MD-11 production for up to six months next year if the company does not receive sufficient orders this year to maintain the flow (*AW&ST* Sept. 19, 1994, p. 56).

However, company officials said the action is considered a worst-case option and probably will not be necessary—especially if the expected Saudi aircraft order for Douglas and Boeing transports is completed in time.

There were only four trijets delivered during the fourth quarter of last year, and only 17 the entire year. Thirty-six MD-11s were delivered during 1993.

DASA, RUSSIA SIGN PACT

PARIS

Daimler-Benz Aerospace and Aviapribor, the major Russian avionics company, are forming a new joint venture to produce and market Western class avionics and air traffic control systems in Russia.

The initiative is designed to enable Daimler-Benz (DASA) to penetrate what German officials believe could be a large market for Western-class avionics in Russia and other parts of the former USSR as vintage Soviet aircraft are modified or replaced.

The new German/Russian alliance will be called Davia and be registered as a joint stock company under Russian law with each of the parent companies holding a 50% share of the new organization's capital. A new production plant in Russia is planned as part of the venture.

IN ADDITION to the sale of basic avionics in Russia, DASA expects other "spin-offs in the development of modern avionics systems" to result from the alliance, according to Jurgen Dangel, president of the Daimler-Benz Sensor System Div.

Likewise, Russian managers hope the new alliance with DASA will enable them to gain greater penetration into existing Western markets outside of the former Soviet Union, according to Sergei Krjukov, Aviapribor president.

Davia managers eventually hope to produce a range of both ground and aircraft navigation and air traffic control equipment. If successful, the new company could compete on its home territory for new Russian air traffic control modernization projects that have previously been dominated by French, U. S. and Italian manufacturers.

Initially, however, the company will focus on marketing Global Positioning System (GPS) receivers and a new aircraft navigation management system planned to be available in 1996. The new company also plans development of a new helicopter avionics suite for Kamov.

The initial capital for the partnership totals about $600,000. A Moscow-based office to initiate the new company will be staffed by 10 persons, headed by a joint German/Russian management staff.

In a related move, DASA is forming a new joint venture with Rockwell International, Seal Beach, Calif., to pursue development and marketing of satellite-based guidance systems and other avionics products. Rockwell's Collins Commercial Avionics division, Cedar Rapids, Iowa, will be the primary U.S. partner in the venture, which DASA expects to be part of its Russian strategy.

Figure 164 Newspaper article describing the FBI's sting operation, including the role that George played in the case.

The United States of America v George Lisenko (version 2)

First of all, we were not brokers, only simple businessmen trying to make a living, so this was a total lie on the FBI part. Omni got a call from a lady named Linda who said that she was starting a business and wanted to know if we were able to sell two bushings from a Douglas blueprint for Landing gear. Well, Linda turned out to be an under Covered FBI agent. They rated Omni Machine to get to the main person who was from D&D Air, who was a Broker and sold spare parts to the airlines without the approval of the FAA, so he falsified the papers on his end, stating that they went through the FAA which they did not. However, we had absolutely nothing to do with him, never met the men, and simply sold him extra parts. We didn't need to be FAA approved because we sold parts to second-tier companies, which were all approved by the FAA, and we were protected under their umbrella. The FBI did everything possible to tie us together to D&D Air, which we had nothing to do with them. Why would we plead guilty to something we didn't do? The answer is simple, The FBI threatened us with a $250,000 fine and 5 years in prison. I decided to plead not guilty however they made it clear to me that my partner Danny would testify against me, even though he knew that we had nothing to do with the FAA and he didn't know about it (I guess he was shaking in his boots and decided to make a deal with the FBI). I couldn't take that chance for my family and company, and I had to plead guilty. Unfortunately, he was my best friend. We went to Vietnam together. He was my best man at my wedding, and his wife was my wife's childhood friend from Peru.   Obviously, that broke my and his friends to this day. My brother in Law, Henry Nahal, who is a Lawyer for the State of New York (who cannot represent me for having a New York license and not a California one), said to me, "If I'm your lawyer, I'm sure I can get you off the hook by Stating that this was a total case of entrapment, for they came to me under false pretenses." Having said that, he also said if I were the prosecutor, I would say, "Ladies and gentlemen of the jury, how would you like to fly 30,000 feet in the air with a part not approved by the FAA?" Even though the two parts sold to the undercover FBI agent were 100% per blueprint.

Potent Omni and the Rising Bottom Line

My secretary eventually moved on, and my daughter, Lynne, took over. We started making money hand-over-fist, as they say, so we were able to hire more workers and also added a night shift. It seemed like every week, Lynne came to me and said, "Dad, I just added $800 to our savings." And the next week, "Dad, I just added $2,000." And the following week, "Dad, I just added another $1,000." And this went on, and on, and on. We were on a serious roll, and we were getting very busy. When my son, Lenny, was 14 years old, I hired him. By that age, he was becoming a pretty good machinist. Lynne and I started discussing buying a building for the shop since Lynne had managed to put away $500,000 in the bank. We started looking for our own building, and a month or so later, we found a building in Santa Fe Springs, CA. The building was listed at somewhere around $750,000, and we put $240,000 down.

At one point in time, I had 4 of my 5 kids working at Omni Machine Corporation. By then, we had great health insurance as well as a retirement plan for our employees. We moved to our new building in October 1999, and we had signed for a 30-year-mortgage, but Lynne was able to get it down to a 10-year-mortgage, which we were able to pay off. Ana was working for an aerospace company at the time that we moved to our new building, and once we paid off our house, Ana quit her job in order to take care of her mother.

One day, I woke up and decided to buy my beautiful wife a diamond ring for no reason other than the fact that I love her. So, I called my friend, Johnny, and his wife, Brenda. She had more diamond rings than any lady I know, and Johnny just kept buying them for her because he could. Anyways, I asked them to go with me and pretend to buy her one more, so Ana and I met them at a jewelry store and told the two girls to pick out a ring. I said, "Honey do you like it?" Ana said, "Yes." I said, "Surprise, it's yours unless you prefer a new car." Ana said, "I'll take the ring!" It was 4 carats on top and 4 carats on the sides. As they say, diamonds are a girl's best friend!

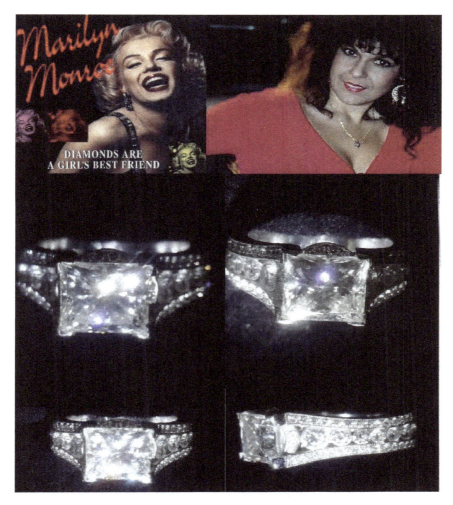

Figure 165 The ring that George bought for Ana.

In 2006, my wife said to me, "Honey, take a look out of the window." I looked out, and there was Nick, Niki's boyfriend, in front of our house to pick her up in a 1962 Chevy Impala convertible. Nick and Niki were both 18 years old at the time. I told Nick, "Nice ride." Nick replied, "It's my dad's; he buys and sells cars. I said, "If your dad ever runs across a 1969 Plymouth GTX 440, let me know." Nick replied, "He just picked one up." I said, "Not a GTO, but a GTX." Nick replied, "That's what he has." I told Nick, "Call your dad. I am interested in the car." I spoke with Nick's dad and asked him if he could bring the car to my house, and he did. As soon as I saw the car coming down the street, I knew I had to have it since I had one back in the day. The bottom line was: I got the car for $20,000 from Javier, Nick's dad, who helped me restore it 100 percent. Javier told me that the guy who owned the car had it in his garage for 35 years without moving it, and the body was in perfect shape. I put hot cam oversized pistons into it, added a six-pack manifold (that's 6 carburetors), redid the interior, and had the exterior painted. All in all, I spent over $30,000 on the car and the restoration. In the first few years of taking the car to shows, I won 28 trophies for the best paint and best engine, as well as 1st place in different car shows. I have put less than 10,000 miles on the car to date. This is a keeper, and I want my son to end up with it.

Figure 166 1969 Plymouth GTX 440

Figure 167 George Lisenko with 1969 Plymouth GTX 440

Figure 168 1969 Plymouth GTX 440

In 2015, we had a deal with Goodrich, a major Aerospace supplier for landing gear. Omni was awarded a 5-million-dollar contract over 4 years. We made some 90 percent of the parts in-house, and we sent about 10 percent of our work to S&S Precision since they have been making these same parts for Omni for many years. S&S Precision made piston rings for all commercial planes, as well as military planes. 99 percent of the blueprints were made one way, but somehow, an engineer drew one backwards. S&S Precision sold us thousands of piston rings over the years and had a 100 percent quality record. We got one job rejected, and Dave and I felt that it was their fault because of the blueprints. The bottom line was that their error cost us over $100,000 dollars. The one thing to learn here is that the big guys are always right, even if they are wrong, and you just can't win when they have all of the money in the world. So, we swallowed the error, Omni and S&S Precision split the bill, and we moved on.

The Leftists Ain't Right and MAGA Trumps Them All

The year 2016 was a great year for me as well as my family and friends. We finally got rid of the Anti-American Obama (I still have no idea how so many people voted for a Muslim). The good news is that we elected a true American, born and raised here in the good old US of A, President Donald Trump. He was and is simply the best of the best. President Trump will go down in history as one of the best presidents ever to have served, while Obama will be somewhere at the bottom. The worst president, by far, will be Traitor Joe. He earned this name by doing more damage in his first year as president than any other president in the history of the United States: he opened up our borders, turned on our Border Patrol (who does that? Traitor Joe does!), turned on I.C.E (who does that? Traitor Joe does!), turned on our police (who does that? Traitor Joe does!), turned on our military (who does that? Traitor Joe does!). I could go on and on, but the question I have is: Who the FUCK voted for this delusional, mental nut job? Talk about a guy that is lost: "Here is my wife" (when it's his daughter), "Welcome, people of Ohio" (when he is in Iowa), "Well, you know what we know about what we know", "Now, we have over 120-MILLION dead from COVID" (when, really, the number was 120-thousand), "If you have a problem figuring out whether you're for Trump or me, then you ain't black." Who in their right mind says this stupid stuff? The answer is Traitor Joe, who also hands out billions of taxpayer dollars to the illegals in aid while our homeless suffer from hunger, and our military veterans are begging for money on the street corners. Traitor Joe earned his name by giving away planes, guns, night vision goggles, aircraft, armed vehicles, sophisticated defense systems, rocket artillery, and mortar rounds to the tune of some $ 83 billion dollars (though no one really knows how much was left behind in Afghanistan). He truly belongs in a nut house, not the White House. Once again, I ask: "Who the FUCK voted for this basket case, and why? The Democratic Party was for the working man back in the 40s, 50s, and 60s, and somewhere along the way, they lost their way. Today, they represent evil, hatred, and protests, where they burn down as much as they can and steal as much as they can from hard-working people. They spit on people, stab horses, overturn police cars, break windows, tear down historical statues, take MY tax money and give it to the illegals. For them, it's all about getting their FREE SHIT. If you are a liberal democratic rat and belong to the mob, how can you sleep at night? Someone needs to open an investigation into the Democrat Party to find out if they have any ties to organizations that are against America.

President Donald Trump always put America first, told NATO to pay their fair share, told China that it's time for them to pay up, got our military back up to speed, got the VA to help take care of our military veterans, had the illegals come through the front door instead of the backdoor. Under President Donald Trump, we had a great economy, great tax cuts, opened up the pipelines, and became friends with Russia (a good thing). Under Traitor Joe Biden, our pipelines were closed, China is now our biggest threat, and Biden and the democrats are clearly back in bed with them.

Figure 169 Political cartoon depicting corrupt politicians, which are mostly Democrats.

Figure 170 President Obama and Vice President Biden, who later became president, as well.

Figure 171 Corrupt politicians.

Figure 172 Donald Trump - 45th President of the United States of America - January 20, 2017 - January 20, 2021 - The Trump family: A true American success story

Looking Back

Looking back to when I first opened the shop, many good and bad things happened. I hired Tom Long to run my shipping department. He also worked for me at my previous job, and we are still good friends, even though he moved on to another job. I also hired a man named Chuck Martinez, and one day, I had an envelope with $27,000 cash in it. I went to my truck, which was parked in front of my shop door, threw my jacket into the passenger side of the door, and left. By the time I arrived home, the envelope was gone! I called the shop, and I had my son retrace my steps to see if he could find the envelope, but he found nothing. The next morning, I came to work, and it turned out that Chuck had found the envelope by the street curb near the shop. The money was all there when he returned it to me. As it turns out, when I threw my jacket into the front seat, the envelope fell out. I was very lucky to have had the envelope returned to me by Chuck since I planned to use it to buy another machine.

I had lots of good times over the years: I had some great parties, I gave away lots of money, I had TVs, stereos, and just lots of STUFF. But, owning a business comes with a high price, as I never expected to be a father, counselor, banker, and so on. My employees came to me all the time and told me: "My mother is sick in El Salvador", "I had a car accident", and "I need to buy a house, and I don't have the money for a down payment", and it never stopped.

In Closing

In closing, looking back at my life, I can honestly say that I only regret two things: one is stealing purses from old ladies, and the other is stealing 50 silver dollars from someone's 50th Anniversary party. I am a true believer in "It's meant to be." If I changed any part of my life, I couldn't have my beautiful kids. Hard work is the answer to success. Never give up on your dreams, and never take "no" for an answer. Keep your dream alive. Do not look backward. Always move forward. Always make sure to surround yourself with people who make you laugh, who would never take advantage of you, and also help you when you are in need. They are the ones worth keeping in your life while everyone else is just passing through. Good things will happen as long as you don't give up. My friends and I are living the good life now because of all of the things we did right in the past.

GOD BLESS DONALD TRUMP!!! GOD BLESS THE UNITED STATES OF AMERICA!
(Per Johnny Salas)

Hobbies and Collections

Some of my Hobbies and things I like to collect and just stuff I like. GUNS – OLD CARS –COINS – HARD ROCK PINS from our travails from around the World – Miniature liquor bottles, and I guess you could call me a guy that likes STUFF.

Figure 173 Small part of my gun collection

Figure 174 Gun shed

Figure 175 Pistol collection

Figure 176 WWII pistols

Figure 177 The Gun I'm holding is one of the Guns my Dad gave to his brother Johnny. The pistol is a P38 9mm FROM Walther arms, the main supplier of guns to the German Army during the war. My uncle says this gun is yours and is in his Will.

How to Succeed With an 8th Grade Education by: George Lisenko

Figure 178 Part of my Trump Collection

Figure 179 Silver dollar coin collection. I'm missing 3 coins, the 1893-S, 94P, and 95P.

Figure 180 Part of my Silver collection (Marvel Comics)

Figure 181 Part of my USA Gold Collection

Figure 182 Part of my Gold Coin collection

Figure 183 Russian Silver Coins

Figure 184 Our Miniature Bottle Collection and Schaffer and Vater pieces (all made in Germany and over 100 years old – center cabinet)

Figure 185 Our Hard Rock Pin Collection represents over 100 countries

Figure 186 Part of my collection of signs

Figure 187 License Plates from 46 different United States and 51 from other countries so far that I have visited

Figure 188 Coca-Cola Sign, trash can, and bottle dispenser.

Figure 189 This is an original 1930's scale

Figure 190 I MAY BE THE ONLY ONE that has a working phone booth in his backyard. As a matter of fact, I have two. I took the 2nd one to the shop and converted it into a shower, and had them both for over 30 years!

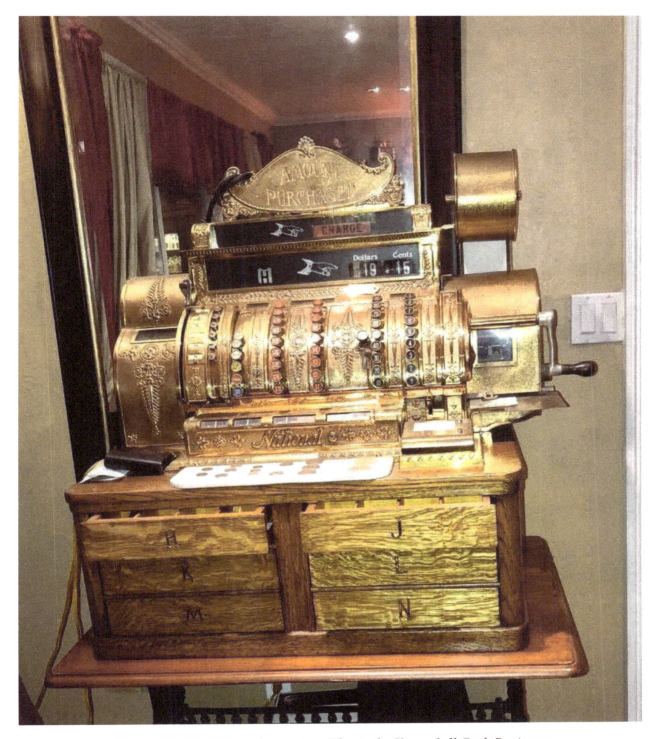

Figure 191 My 1915 cash register – This is the King of all Cash Registers

Figure 192 My jukeboxes

Figure 193 My new additions: Mobil Pegasus and Fire Chief Gas Pumps from the 1940s. Bought the Fire Chief Gas pump for Jonathan Hanna, my son-in-law, for he is a Fireman.

Family and Friends

Figure 194 One of my favorite pictures of my daughter Lynne

Figure 195 Ana and Angel, Brenda and Johnny, Manil and Sanjiv, Carlos and Angie, and friends having fun. Carlos, out of Chicago from Peru, has been my good friend for many years me and him had lots of good times in my bottle collecting years.

Figure 196 Amy has been a good friend for over 30 years Beautiful then and Beautiful now. She sold me Metal for my shop she was and is in sells at the FRY STEEL CO.

Figure 197 Ana's friends Roxana and Lili

Figure 198 The Bonilla Family: Patty, Laura, and Yolanda (mom)

Figure 199 Bob and Patty – we have been friends for 38 years. Bob and Paddy had a very successful insurance business – Bob from New York and Paddy from Peru. She and Ana went to a Catholic school together in Lima, Peru.

Figure 200 Our closest dear friends: Johnny and Brenda and their beautiful family and two of his cars. He also has a 1961 ragtop (convertible) as well as 5 Jukeboxes and 9 Cash registers, and just lots of stuff. Javier and Maria and family with his 1958 Chevy Impala and has flipped over 100 1950s and 60s cars, including my GTX.

Figure 201 Johnny, Brenda, and their kids.

Figure 202 My daughter Lynne, Debbie, Roxana, Carina, and John

Figure 203 George's cousin Albert Abda (son of John Abda, Jr.), and George

Figure 204 Lisa, Nancy, Albert, Joe, Johnny, Will, Diamond, and James (Love this picture)

Figure 205 James, William, Albert, Johnny, and Joe

Figure 206 (Left to right): Grandpa John, Grandma Diamond, and their five boys, Joseph, Johnny, William, Albert, and James.

Figure 207 Lisa, Johnny, Nancy, Aaron, and Tara

Figure 208 Albert, Rosemary, Thea, Jim, Tara, Aaron, Dennis, John, Henry James

Figure 209 Johnny, Lisa, Al, Lynne, Jim, Denise, Alexis, and Nancy.

Figure 210 Tara's wedding day, with Aaron driving my Dad's 1948 Chrysler.

Figure 211 Lenny and Lauren; John, Stephanie, Janis, and Rene; Albert; Niki and Alex; Victor, Kim, Olga, and Jim; Our family; Lynne; Alexis, Richy, Denise; George, Ana, and Kathy; Melissa; Kaylan; Stephanie and kids

Figure 212 Lisa and Johnny; Albert and George; Lisa; Johnny, Albert, and kids

Figure 213 My picture as a Veteran was posted on the wall at the Veterans Administration Hospital in Long Beach, CA. Where the Hell did all the years go? As my Mom used to say, it SUCKS getting older. Boy, ain't that the truth?

Figure 214 Ronny, Jimmy, and Richard; John, Rene, Janis and Stephanie; Sandra and Jay; Ashley and Lauren; The Davis Family, Lenny, and Denise; The Lisenko family; Erica, Galina, and Rebecca; Jim and Olga; Melissa and Christina

Figure 215 William, Joe, Johnny, James, and Albert

Figure 216 George and Lenny

Figure 217 Ana and George

Figure 218 Alex, Niki, Ana, and George

Figure 219 Righteous Brothers Concert – Ana, George, Maria, Bill Medley, Brenda, Johnny, and Javier (2010)

Figure 220 Niki

As the years went by, our daughters Alex and Niki graduated High School and moved on to College. Alex graduated from Cal State University, Fullerton, in 2011, and Niki from Cal State University, Long Beach, in 2012

Figure 221 Alex

Figure 222 Niki

Figure 223 Our Family picture

Figure 224 Niki and her friends out having a good time in Texas.

Figure 225 My NIKI is fully loaded, all 5 of my kids love Guns, I guess it helps to be very Conserved. I took my kids out to the desert at an early age to go shooting, and they loved it.

I must say I'm not sure why but I am truly blessed with a Beautiful wife and 5 great-looking kids, and a large loving family. What more can a man ask for?

Figure 226 Uncle Johnny and George

I am very fortunate to have 4 uncles, I love them all, but Uncle Johnny is my favorite. I have stayed in contact with him since 1986 till this day. He has by far one of the best gun collections out there. I couldn't count them all. All I know is he has a SHIT load of them. When my Father returned from Germany at the end of WWII, he somehow managed to bring home 4 different guns, and one of them was the 1911 .45 caliber standard military issue. My dad gave them all to his brother Johnny who in turn gave me the .45 pistol. It means a lot to me. I have a picture of my mom holding the .45 (my sister Denise gave me the pictures of my DAD HAD). I gave the gun to my son Lenny.

Figure 227 .45 caliber 1911 that Albert Abda brought home from WWII.

Figure 228 My son Lenny's pictures

Figure 229 Lenny, his Mom Lelah, and Lynne

Figure 230 Lenny and his Beautiful wife, Denise

Figure 231 Lynne and Lenny

Figure 232 Denise and Lenny's wedding day

Figure 233 Denise and Lenny saying their wedding vows

Figure 234 Denise and Lenny's wedding reception

Figure 235 Lenny's daughter Lauren and Smokey, our family horse, have been with us for 35 years

Figure 236 Me and my beautiful granddaughter Lauren

Figure 237 Sister Olga and family

Figure 238 My brother Victor and family

Figure 239 My sister Frieda and family (with Aunt Nina)

Figure 240 My sister Denise and family

Figure 241 My sister Alexis and family and my dad's 1948 Town and Country Chrysler, bottom picture with Uncle Johnny.

Figure 242 My two sisters came to visit California, and with Ana, they are enjoying the jacuzzi.

Figure 243 The Davis and Nahal families are so happy to be part of these Beautiful Families!

Figure 244 David Mosier and his granddaughters, Fiona and Olivia.

Figure 245 Lisa The Crazy Dog Lady is one of my first Cousins and one of my favorites. She is a very hard-working dog groomer and is providing herself a very good livening and is fun to B.S. with.

Figure 246 Sandra King (Abda), her husband Jay King, and their kids

Figure 247 Cousins Richard and Lauren (Richard was the first cousin I met that came to California)

Figure 248 Uncle Johnny's 3 kids, Rene, Stephanie, and John

Figure 249 My grandson, Trevor Goldyn

Figure 250 Trevor in USMC uniform

My grandson Trevor joined the marines for a 5-year term. He was in his 5th year when he was stationed in Bahrain and made the rank of Sargent when sadly, he was killed there in 2020.

Figure 251 Trevor on active duty and as a senior in high school

Figure 252 Abda family

Third row: *Robin's daughter –William Santarsiero-Ana Lisenko-Johnny Abda, George Lisenko-Lisa Abda -Al Abda -Billy Abda, and William Abda*

Second row: *Cheryl Simon – Robin Rowlands Pliss- Kaylee Harrity*

Front row: *Mitchel Simon – Henry Nahal –Denise Abda Nahal –Alexis Abda Davis – Kim Abda Santarsiero – Kim Abda Harrity*

Figure 253 My first cousin Sandra and her husband Jay, who sadly passed away.

Figure 254 My cousin Richard with my niece Ashley on her wedding day

Figure 255 Uncle Johnny and I are visiting the Abda's graves in Scranton, PA

Figure 256 Abda's uncles and Grandma Diamond.

Favorite Movies

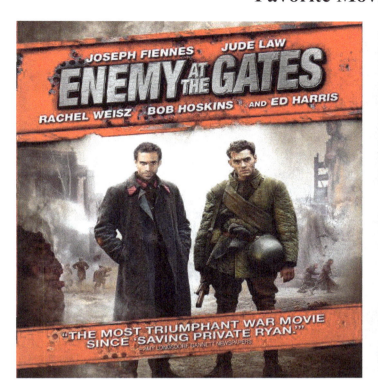
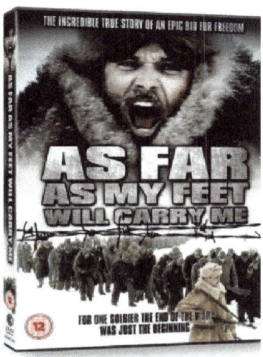
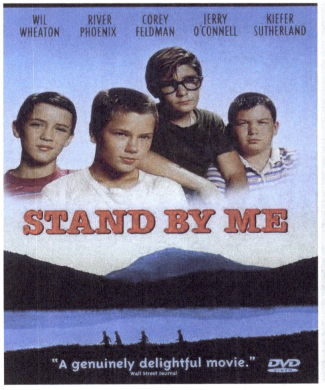

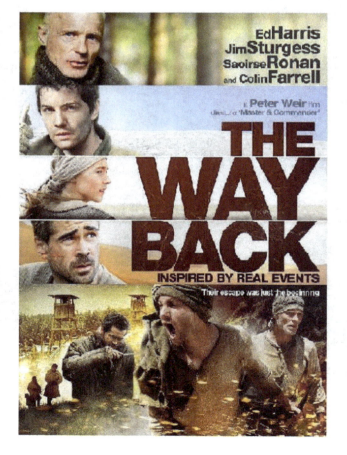

Stories from Others

From Frieda

Granddad, George Lisenko, was an educated man and was an accountant by profession. Nina, my grandmother, was a lady, and they lived a comfortable life during the Tsar's reign. They generally had a live-in maid, usually, a young girl from a nearby village, who performed all domestic chores in the home. My mother was the only child. During the turmoil in Russia, my granddad joined the White Army to fight against the Bolsheviks. Sometime in 1943, in Pyatigorsk, Russia, my mother met Heinz Kessel, a German soldier. They became friends in the atmosphere of daily bombings between the Russians and Germans. Most of the time, they felt that this might be their last night alive on this earth. When the Germans started to retreat, they provided train transportation to Germany for Russian citizens with German blood lines, such as my grandmother Nina. They were treated more humanely than other refugees during that time. My mother and her parents left their home and all of their belongings to immigrate to Germany to avoid being persecuted by the Red Army soldiers.

From Jim and Alexis

Denise has perfectly described our lives together. I will try to fill you in with a few things that stand out in my life. Jim showed up in my life as his family became tenants to my great grandmother, Rose Haddad, in a 2-bedroom apartment that was two houses removed from where I lived. We were just kids at that time. Jim and I had a common love, which was the "Woodie" Chrysler convertible. My parents purchased the car in 1948 from a Chrysler dealer in East Stroudsburg, PA, for $3,300 with money that they received from their wedding in September of 1946 and my father-in-law's army pay after serving in World War II as a driver of an armored car carrier.

The Chrysler was stored in our garage and had not been driven for a few years as the fuel pump broke. In any event, Jim helped my father-in-law install the fuel pump, and the car was now operable. In the spring of 62', Jim and I got the urge to start up the Chrysler. We got into the car, started it up, and drove around the block to pass in front of my in-law's grocery store, which stood agape as we went by and blew the horn. Jim and I were now in love with the Chrysler, and we went everywhere in it; to my Senior Prom, to the beach, cruising around the city of Scranton with the top down, etc.

Also, at that time, my grandmother, Bertha "Bert" Dennis, who lived in Asbury Park, NJ, needed a car just for the summer months to drive Denise and me to the beach from their house (15 blocks from the ocean). But, first, Bert had to pass her driver's test. Jim taught both of us how to drive, and we both passed our driver's test with the Chrysler.

My next stop was Monmouth College in New Jersey in 1965, living with my grandparents. Jim was working on his doctorate degree at Lehigh at that time. Jim would hitchhike from Bethlehem, PA, to New Jersey every weekend and would always have fun stories to share about the people who would give him a ride. Of course, hitch-hiking is something you would not think of doing today, but at that time, it was a valid means of transportation. We enjoyed many weekends with "Bert and Pop" in Asbury Park, New Jersey.

We married on June 28, 1968 (last weekend in June to be a "June bride"), and Jim continued hitchhiking to see me until I graduated from Monmouth College with a degree in teaching in 1969. We then settled down in Hellertown, PA, which is near Lehigh University, until Jim received his doctorate in chemistry while I received my Master's degree as well in 1972. During this time, I taught elementary education at Saucon Valley School District.

After receiving his doctorate degree, Jim sent out hundreds of applications for employment. The NASA space program was shut down, putting thousands of doctoral students in the market for a job, so there was a lack of available positions. Jim finally received ONE offer at a firm called Amchem, and he took it. Since Amchem was located in Ambler, PA, we moved to our current location in North Wales, PA, in 1976. This was an ideal location for us, as it is close to both Scranton, where Jim's family also lives, and Asbury Park.

The next ten years were extremely busy for us. Thea was born in 1972, John was born in 1974, Aaron was born in 1976, and Tara was born in 1978. Additionally, Jim traveled the world with his job, helped my family when he could, and we spent our holidays in Scranton and Asbury Park. Thea and John were born in Scranton, which was a blessing for us, and the kids were enjoyed by my dad and mom, my grandparents (Bert and Pop), my grandmother (Diamond Abda), my father's brothers, Jim's parents (Lucile and William Davis), Jim's siblings (Irene, Keith, and Madeleine), and friends and other relatives, who all remain close to this day.

Our lives were turned upside down when my father became ill in 1984 and passed away in 1986, followed by my mother's illness from the day my father passed away until her death in 1996. During this period, with the help of Henry, Jim, and Uncle James's oldest son, "Jimmy", the properties were maintained. Denise and I shared my mother's caretaking during her very painful illness. We were happy to have been able to take her to visit George, which she wanted to do.

Jim and I have been blessed in our lives with four kinds, loving children and their spouses, who are the best sons-in-law that anyone could ask for. John lives the closest to us, which is a blessing as we get older. Aaron became a California guy and helped George in his business at Omni. Aaron has two great boys, Owen and Eli, and now lives in Benicia and has become close to George and his family. Thea and Rob live about 45 minutes from us and have three smart and loving girls, Kayla, Carolyn, and Allison. Tara and Lew live in Goshen, NY, and have three beautiful, smart children, Eva, Violet, and Lewis. In summary, we are thankful for George contacting us about his relationship with our father. We are saddened that George never met my father in person to truly get to know how wonderful a man he was.

I have included a few pictures for potential use in your book (see below).

Figure 257 Jim and Alexis at their wedding

Figure 258 Jim and Alexis's wedding reception

From Denise

Well, brother, you asked for a "paragraph" about my life, so here goes. I was born in Scranton, Pennsylvania, on June 14, 1950. My mother, Rose Marie Dennis Abda, shared a hospital room with my aunt Charlotte, who was married to my father, Albert Abda's, brother, James. Aunt Charlotte delivered my first cousin, James Abda Jr., on that same day. I was baptized not long after at St. Joseph's Melkite Church in a beautiful satin gown that my parents ordered when my sister, Alexis, was born two-and-a-half years earlier on December 11, 1947. The three-piece gown was hand-made by cloister nuns who lived in a remote area on the east mountain in Scranton. I remember my dad telling us about how he slipped the silky, satin fabric (as well as some candy and cigarettes) through a letter slot in the door of the convent. The nuns sewed the fabric into an exquisite cape, gown, and slip. This christening gown was worn by most of the newborn babies in the Abda/Haddad families, a tradition that continues today!

Figure 259 The Christening gowns! Henry and Mason are in the gown and slip made by the cloister nuns.

Pennsylvania was not to be my home for the first five years of my life. My mother accidentally burned her arm while cooking, and the burn rendered her in need of help. So, her parents, Bertha Haddad Dennis and Foster Merrel Dennis took me to New Jersey for a "brief" stay. That "brief" stay turned into five years. I'm told because my grandparents were lonely in New Jersey. They had just moved there from Scranton for my grandfather's work with the federal government as an electrical engineer. This is where my grandfather would later help to develop the first portable handheld radar that would be used by infantry troops in battle, a tracking radar to shoot down incoming rockets and missiles, and many electronics that allowed people to have color TV.

Figure 260 This is me in front of my grandparent's home in Wanamassa, New Jersey

My grandparents left Scranton with one suitcase between them, leaving the apartment they lived into my mom and dad, as well as a grocery store to manage (which previously belonged to my great grandmother, Rose Risk Haddad). Grandma and Grandpa Haddad lived right next door, as did most of the family! They all helped my mom with my sister, Alexis. My mom was an only child, but she had many cousins who lived close by, and we remain close to all of these families to this day. My mom was very dedicated to her grandmother, helping her with her youngest daughter, Isabell Haddad, who was sick and needed care.

Figure 261 My mom and her grandmother in front of our church, St. Joseph's Melkite, in Scranton, PA

Meanwhile, I enjoyed being spoiled while I was living with my grandparents in New Jersey! We were always together for every important life event. We were in Scranton for Thanksgiving and Christmas and in New Jersey for the Easter parade at the Ashbury Park boardwalk, of course.

Figure 262 the Year 1958 - Christmas in Scranton, PA

Back in Scranton, our parents were busy raising my sister, Alexis, working very hard managing the grocery store and purchasing/managing rental properties.

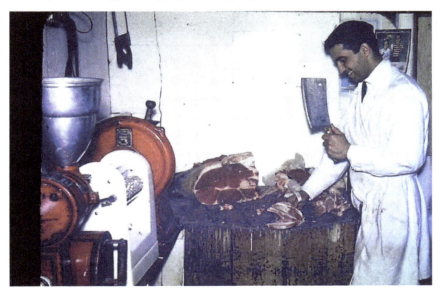

Figure 263 Dad, the butcher!

At age 5, my father insisted that I come back to Scranton to go to school. I remember being told that he was worried that I wouldn't even know my sister.

Figure 264 Alexis and I

I returned to Scranton and attended Lincoln Elementary School. I entered kindergarten with a broken arm, as I had fallen on my daily run to meet my grandfather at the corner at 5:15 pm (the exact time he would come home from work every single day). I loved my grandparents and enjoyed living with them. During this time, Dad was busy building the house, which we still own, on the land next to Grandma and Grandpa Haddad's house.

Figure 265 My favorite room in the house my dad built

My grandmother said it was OK for me to go back to Scranton, but only if Alexis and I would spend every summer in New Jersey. To this day, we still spend every summer in that very house. Even now, we love being there with our 10 families, treasuring the beautiful memories of being there with our grandparents. When Alexis and I were summering in New Jersey, our parents would save every penny and put a down payment on another rental property. Our summer days were spent swimming in the Atlantic Ocean and enjoying the beautiful Ashberry Park beach. For several years, we were lucky enough to be members of the Monte Carlo Pool and Beach Club. This Monte Carlo had the largest saltwater pool in the world at the time. The beach club also offered beautiful cabanas, lockers, a restaurant, and a tunnel that extended from the pool to underneath Ocean Avenue and straight to the beach. Of course, it also had a high dive pool (where I spent countless hours), as well as a kiddie pool. My grandmother paid for the membership, and our next-door neighbor, Madeline Dello, drove us and her children, Linda, Michael, Peter, and Mary, back and forth every day. Sadly, due to racial tensions in the 1960s, the Monte Carlo was closed down for good. However, the Dellos remains our oldest and dearest friends.

Figure 266 The Monte Carlo in Ashbury Park, NJ

Elementary school in Scranton, NJ, was great. I loved school and made up my mind right then that I wanted to be a teacher. My father encouraged this goal; he told me that he would want me to be his teacher and also said, "You'll be able to raise your family." I remember these words and treasure them. Dad gave me a door-sized slate board and leaned it against the wall in our basement. I started teaching there at around age 9 or 10 years old, helping a special needs neighbor with his school work!

My sister, Alexis, met Jim Davis when I was about 11 years old. Jim's family rented an apartment above our grocery store. Alexis and Jim were a huge part of my life, and as I said before, our parents worked very hard every day. Therefore, Jim and Alexis basically became "parents" to me. Jim taught me how to drive in our parents' 1948 Chrysler that my parents bought right out of the factory while on their honeymoon. Additionally, Alexis was the best role model and the greatest influence in my life. Their guidance got me through West 13 High School, where Jim would help me with my school work, especially chemistry! Jim Davis was and always has been there for all of us. He worked his way through school, achieving his doctoral degree in chemistry while helping our dad with the grocery store and rental apartments. In addition to all of that, he also hitchhiked to New Jersey on summer weekends to see his love, Alexis.

Figure 267 Jim and Alexis with their children, Thea, John, Aaron, and Tara

I joined the marching band at West Scranton Senior High and played the saxophone for six years at every football game, graduation, and school event. I never missed a day of school; I loved learning and still do. I attended East Stroudsburg State Teacher's College from 1968 to 1972, and upon graduation, I packed my car and moved back to my grandparents' home in New Jersey. It's funny, but I don't even recall thinking about going back to Scranton. It's not that I didn't love Scranton, as I have many wonderful memories there, especially at Christmas when we shopped in the Globe store. But my heart was in New Jersey with my grandparents.

Figure 268 An incredible New York-style department store

My grandparents' story was a true love story. After Foster graduated from Penn State in 1923, he and Bertha eloped.

Figure 269 From left to right - Foster & Bertha Dennis, Diamond & John Abda – Picture taken on our parents' wedding day

You see, Foster was not Lebanese, and Grandma Haddad would not approve of their relationship. Eventually, their marriage was accepted, and Foster was loved and respected by all of the family. I loved my father's parents, John and Diamond Abda, dearly, but I didn't get to spend much time with them. They were hard-working and loving grandparents.

Figure 270 Diamond, on the far right, with her 8 sisters, and her mother is front and center

Grandpa Abda was born in Lebanon, and Granny Abda was born in America and was one of 12 children. Once in a while, we would go to Granny and Grandpa Abda's home for Sunday dinner, and we would be together with all of the cousins, uncles, and aunts. Grandpa Abda would make the largest and most amazing salad, as well as Kibbee, which was the national dish of Lebanon. Grandpa Abda was 60 years old when he passed away.

Figure 271 Grandpa and Granny Abda, along with their five sons: Joseph, William, Albert, James, and John, who all lived in or around Scranton.

Dad, along with his two older brothers, and his two younger brothers, seemed to me to become the heart of the family. He stayed close to his brothers, helping each of them at a second's notice. Our uncles, who called themselves the WAJJJ, as well as their wives, were the best uncles and aunts that anyone could ask for. Uncle James's family lived a few blocks from our house. We attended school with Jim, Richard, and Ronnie. Richard and I enjoyed lots of weekends "hanging out" in and around the West Side. Our cousin, Jim, helped dad deliver groceries on weekends, and dad helped Jim build his own home. Later, Jim helped us maintain the properties that we inherited in Scranton. One of my fondest memories was around the holidays during the days between Christmas and New Year's when we would visit each of our uncle's homes. They all had wonderful Christmas trees, elaborate train setups, holiday treats, and beautiful decorations. We loved every moment with our cousins. That is what Christmas means to me, even today: love and family. Though we are no longer close in proximity to each other, we remain as close as ever to all of our cousins and their families.

In September of 1972, I obtained a teaching job in New Jersey. The day before school started, I remember getting a phone call with a woman's voice asking me, "Would you like to come to work tomorrow?" That was my first teaching job and the beginning of my 33 years in education.

I met Henry Nahal, the love of my life, at his cousin's home in Scranton! Henry's aunt lived a block away from my family, and his cousin and I went to the same school. Henry and I had a long-distance relationship for several years, during the time he was finishing up law school. Henry would call frequently, and we would also write letters back and forth to each other. We visited each other whenever it was possible. Henry proposed to me in 1973, and in 1974 we married at Saint Joseph's Melkite Church in Scranton, surrounded by the love and support of all of our friends and family. Father Seraphim Michalenko crowned us King and Queen under the eyes of God, and we have continued to treat each other as such in following our faith each and every day. I can still remember the moment Henry held my hand as we entered the church. I have that same feeling every time he holds my hand. I knew then, as I know now, that we are in this together, and his strength and love are always there. Henry's faith, work ethic, and commitment to helping each client, friend, and family member in need have been amazing to witness for 47 years and counting.

Figure 272 I bought my wedding dress at the Globe store, of course

My maternal grandparents were thrifty and were able to provide us with enough money for a down payment on a home. So, a year after we married, we moved out of our small apartment in Guilderland, New York, into our present home in East Greenbush. We have been here for 47 years. It's here, with the love, help, and support of Henry's parents, Henry and Marjorie Nahal, who lived in Troy, New York, that we raised our two wonderful sons, Dennis Albert Nahal and Henry James Nahal.

Figure 273 Henry's Parents Henry and Marjorie Nahal, on their 50th Wedding anniversary

Henry coached many of their baseball teams, and together, we continue coaching them through life. We could not be prouder of the fine young men they have become. The older we get, the more often it is that Dennis and Henry end up "coaching us". Both of our boys live in our area, which we thank God for every day. They are loving, caring, kind-hearted, and successful young men.

Figure 274 Our blessing in life

In June of 1986, our hearts were broken when we lost our beloved father. He died from a reaction to a chemotherapy drug that he was taking to treat his non-Hodgkin lymphoma. Three priests concelebrated his funeral mass at his beloved St. Joseph Melkite Church. Our dad had unwavering faith, with a strong devotion to St. Ann. He told us that when he was in high school, he was suffering from painful boils on his back. The night before his school prom, he prayed to St. Ann, and she healed him completely that very night. Dad attended mass every Sunday in his best dress suit and was dedicated to helping every priest that was assigned to our church. You see, his father had helped build that church when he came to America from Lebanon. Henry often retells a story about the time when the priest wanted a ceiling lightbulb replaced but had no ladder available to reach the high ceiling. Dad called upon Henry and Jim to come over to the church to help. Jim and Henry held the ladder in the air, and Dad climbed the ladder to replace the bulb! Dad's faith never faltered through the ups and downs of life. With broken hearts, we buried him on my birthday, June 14, 1986.

Not long after that, we met you, my dear brother. And, talk about a blessing! I can never express how thankful we are to have you and your beautiful family in our lives. The "war story", as Uncle James referred to it, which brought you to us, is what brought all of us together. We are ever so thankful for you, dear brother; ever so thankful for the example you have set for us with your love and dedication to all of your family.

Our mother passed on in 1996. After Dad died, she was diagnosed with an autoimmune disease called polymyositis. I sometimes think that a broken heart was the cause, as she suffered through this debilitating condition for 10 years.

Our son, Henry James, married his beautiful wife, Megan McLaughlin, in 2008 and gave us three amazing grandchildren: Henry Ryan, Mason Dennis, and Charlotte. Dennis and Rebecca Armsby also gave us two "grandchildren", Connor and Carter Dee, who are Rebecca's children. We love them like they are our own. In a blink of an eye, we find ourselves in our 70s, now treasuring every moment that life presents us with. We know how precious each moment is, and we thank God for every moment.

From Olga

Here is my life in a nutshell.... the details are as I remember, but not necessarily the true facts.

My name is Olga Faszczuk Dilenge, and I was born on the kitchen table of the apartment I lived in with my parents, my older sister, and my brother in Erlangen, Germany, on March 10, 1955. My siblings are Frieda, who I believe was 10 at the time of my birth, and George, who I believe was 8. My mom was a product of the war with a broken heart, given to her one true love, my brother, George's father. I found all of this out way later when I was in my teens. My sister, Frieda's dad, was a German man that my mom knew briefly. In my opinion, she only married my dad to give George and Frieda a father and herself a stable life. Unfortunately, my dad was a terrible father to Frieda and George because they weren't 'his'. My mom worked in the Prudential Building in Cush as a cleaner, and my dad worked in a factory. They installed in us a great work ethic. As bad as he was to them, he grew to be ashamed and loved them as his own, but this happened much, much later in life. Because of him, Frieda married young to a wonderful man named Nick, and George enrolled in the Marine Corp. when he was 16 years old. He stayed in California after the service and is there to this day. He never went beyond the 8th grade but showed the world that a person could become extremely successful as long as he or she works hard. My name was always the worst part of my childhood, and I couldn't wait to get married so I could change it! The funny part is that my mom named her dogs Linda and Kelly!

I married a wonderful guy named Jim and had two beautiful daughters: Rebecca and Erica. Funny enough, Rebecca married Jim, too, but he goes by James.

I don't really have many memories of my life, but my stand-out memories were when George came home on leave from the Marines, and I sat on the toilet and watched him shave. It was amazing to me that he shaved not only his face but down his throat! That, and his love of Motown music. He was, and is, my hero!

From Victor

The Book of George

The phone rang at 1:00 pm on December 10, 2021, 2 days before what would have been Dad's 94th birthday. On the phone was my brother George. Calls from George are always interesting. We don't speak often, but when we do, it's always a call that leaves me grateful.

Today's discussion centered on a new project that my brother was undertaking – he wanted to write a book. A book that detailed his life – a memoir that would offer his children, and more importantly, his grandchildren, a glimpse into his life. It seems that George always has a project underway. It would be a very long list if I detailed all of the projects that he worked on (and those are just the ones that I was aware of). Along with projects, my brother is an expert collector. It was easy for me to be influenced by him since he is my older brother. I started many collections as a result of following in George's footsteps.

For this new project – the "Book of George", he asked me if I could write a few paragraphs regarding my thoughts on our family's history as I saw it. I was pleased because I thought it was important to provide my view. You see, I was the youngest of 4 children. Being the youngest, I was certainly gifted with the ability to not only be the brat of the family, but I also got to see everyone go on their own paths as I grew up.

We are a very ethnic family. Mom – Galina, and Dad – Victor, migrated to the United States in February of 1957 from Germany. They landed briefly in New York and quickly established themselves in Chicago, Illinois. My older sister, Frieda, is 14 years older than me. George is 12 years older than me, and the younger of my two sisters, Olga, is 3 years older than me. And, of note: I was the only sibling to be born in the U.S. and the only one to be given a middle name (which would come in handy when I arrived in the 3rd grade). I was born on November 8, 1958. Olga always told me that I was born at Cook County Hospital (the hospital for the indigent) out of sheer jealousy. But, in fact, I was born at Walther Memorial Hospital on Kedzie Ave in Chicago. This was the same hospital where our grandfather on dad's side, Roman Faszczuk, passed away. He died in 1974.

To be fair, even in my earliest memories, I never remembered living under the same roof with Frieda and George. Not only were they older than me, but I think that they both scooted out of the house as early as they could. So, by the time I was 5 years old, they were both gone. Frieda got married to Nick, a man who was capable of researching, repairing, and fixing almost anything in and around the house. He saved my butt when I was about 10 or 11 years old. I had a rifle that shot BBs. One afternoon, I shot the TV. Before dad found out what I did – Frieda took pity on me and had Nick replace the picture tube. His abilities were amazing. Even when I was older and married, when we moved into our first home, I called Nick to help me understand how to install a ceiling fan. I was afraid to mess with electricity, but it was something that Nick was an expert at.

George went into the Marine Corp. at a very early age. I heard his enlistment was at the urging of a Chicago Court Judge. I think George would agree that the Marine Corp. was the best thing for him. George was always my big brother, and that's the way I thought of him. Throughout my life, or at least up to my early thirties, I was sadly not close to him. Early on, when he was in the service, I remember him coming home on leave. He had approximately 2 seconds of time for me before he moved on to anything more interesting than his snot-nosed little brother. I do remember one time when I was in the Cub Scouts, and we had tickets to a Chicago Cubs baseball game. Unknown to George, I volunteered him to be one of the chaperones for a group attending the game. George was nice enough to handle his duties, but I'm sure he spent most of the time at the game looking at girls. I, at least, had the pleasure of showing off my big military brother to my Cub Scout friends.

When I was in the eighth grade, my mom made arrangements that she and I would travel to California, where George was now living as a young married guy. It was my first trip on an airplane. I remember meeting George's first wife, Lelah. She was a really nice lady. They took us to Tijuana, then to Disneyland, then over to visit with Aunt Nina, Dad's younger sister, who lived near George in Whittier, CA. I remember that it was a wonderful trip.

Vacations weren't really a routine for the Faszczuk's. I only remember a couple of trips with my parents. I was fortunate that Frieda made a couple of vacations happen. We would drive over to Indiana to a property that Frieda's in-law's family owned during the summer. We stayed in a small little house on the property for a week or so. It was really a great time. When I was a kid, I didn't appreciate those trips as I should have. As with many things in my life, I didn't obtain a true appreciation until I was far older and looked back on how fortunate I was.

It was during one of these summer vacation trips to the house in Indiana that I learned that what I always thought was my family unit (a mom, dad, two sisters, and a brother) wasn't what I thought. I remember Frieda trying to explain to me that she and George were actually step-siblings. I have no idea what led to this talk, but my guess would be that maybe Frieda felt that I was finally old enough to understand the situation. I think I might have been eight at the time. And, at eight, trying to understand that she and George weren't my full-blood brother and sister was really hard. At that time, that was all I knew. What I did come to learn was that Frieda and George had different dads than Olga and I. It took a little time for this new concept to sink in. But, I can confidently say, regardless of any formal title to the contrary, I always believed Frieda and George were my sister and brother. I never looked at it any other way.

George was my older brother, but since he had a family and lived in California, I never had the chance to share any experiences with him that other brothers may have had growing up with each other. I lived in Chicago. I had my own set of friends and loved being a kid. A life-changing moment occurred for me when I was beginning the seventh grade at Alfred Noble elementary school. I met the person that would turn into the love of my life, Kimberly Chaplin. Kim lived a full neighborhood away from us. But, since her local elementary school only supported kindergarten to sixth grade, she had to transfer to my school to complete seventh and eighth grades. I'm not sure how I managed it, but I did get her to kiss me on the corner during that first year of us being at school together. We dated (what kids called dating) briefly, but I was too young to fully understand how great she was. After eighth grade (1972), Frieda sold the house where we were living. Years earlier, Nick and Frieda bought a two-flat house on Chicago's west side. Frieda, Nick, and their two daughters, Cathy and Laura, lived on the first floor, and Mom, Dad, Olga, and I lived above them. With Nick, Frieda, and their daughters off to a Chicago suburb, Wheeling, IL., mom and dad purchased their first home on Chicago's west side, which was blocks from Oak Park, IL.

I was sad to leave my neighborhood friends, but moving seemed exciting to me. Starting high school while living in the new house made things a bit easier for me. I was not very good at school. All throughout elementary school and the first two years of high school, I earned poor grades. It was hard for me to focus, and I hated reading anything. I finally started taking school seriously in the 11th grade. From that point on, school wasn't a chore. I was accepted into an all-male vocational public high school in Chicago. Kim went to an all-girls Catholic school in Chicago. After eighth grade, I didn't see her very much, but I thought about her all the time. If my parents ever drove near her house, I would always be looking for her. Every once in a while, one of my high school buddies who had a car would drive over to Kim's school to see one of their girlfriends, and I remember always hoping I would run into her. When I finally got my driver's license, on the day of my sixteenth birthday, my mom let me take the day off of school, and she took me to the

DMV to get license. How cool is that?! I would always drive by Kim's house on the way home from anywhere. Kim lived with her family in a large home with an enormous porch on a busy boulevard. Her grandmother and aunt lived above them. And at one point, her aunt and uncle lived below them. I was fortunate because since the house she lived in had a large porch, they would always sit outside and watch what was going on in the neighborhood. They lived across the street from a park, and the church where we would eventually get married was on the corner. But I'm getting ahead of myself.

It was my senior year of high school, and I didn't date much. Admittedly, I was a bit shy. When being a jokester, I was much braver. One on one, I was a shy coward. Kim was always far more outgoing than me. That was probably the main reason that her parents never let her out. She was always grounded for some reason or another. Again, I was blessed, as I don't remember mom and dad ever grounding me. Make no mistake. They would discipline me in other ways; they simply beat the crap out of me. That always got my attention. Dad had a way of grabbing the hair on the side of my ear when he needed my focus. Boy, I remember that really hurt. Senior year – crunch time! I needed to figure out a date for the senior prom. Even though it was months away, I was sweating this every day. The week between Christmas and New Year 1975, we were off from school. I finally mustered the strength and the nerve to call Kim. Thank God that she never moved or changed her phone number. I called – she answered. Wow! We talked; briefly, I knew my limits, and small talk was not a strength. I asked her if she wanted to go to a Beatles movie with me, "A Way with Words," which was more like a documentary. It was being shown at the Shubert Theater in downtown Chicago on January 3, 1976. By the grace of God, she accepted. The magic started.

I got to her house for the night of our first date. Kim answered the door and let me come in. Her father was the first to greet me, and he asked to see the tickets I had for "this movie" we were going to. I had to go back out to the car and get the tickets, but it seemed to satisfy him, and he never asked to see the tickets again. I'm not sure if I ever saw a minute of the film; Kim and I talked the whole time. I mentioned that I was pretty shy. When we went to the movie, several of my friends (friends we still have today) attended as well. After the movie, we all made plans to go to the Comeback Inn for something to eat. Then, I took Kim home. My stomach was flipping. I had the best time of my young life, but I was hoping beyond hope that she had a good time. We all made plans to go out to a new shopping mall that was built in Bolingbrook called "Old

Chicago". It was the first mall to have a small amusement park inside. She again accepted my invitation. We were never apart from that weekend.

Life with Kim was easy and fun. The first awful thing that happened was in March of 1977. Kim's dad, Henry (Hank), died. He was at the house, and he stayed home from work as he wasn't feeling well. He suffered a massive heart attack and never recovered. Kim and I always commented that Hank never got to see and experience so many things. The obvious being our children, but less obvious were things like microwave ovens and cell phones.

Since I went to a vocational high school, the school got me a job at an electric motor company. I started working cleaning parts and made my way up to delivering motors. One day, the company was shorthanded, and they asked me to order some needed items. That was another turning point for me. I entered the world of the white-collar workforce, and I never wanted to go back to cleaning parts. I was lucky that the company gave me the chance to continue working in the office and to learn the administrative side of the business. After high school, I continued to work for the electric motor company. A few years later, my sister, Olga, was working for AT&T. While helping her move one weekend, I had the chance to meet her boss. He offered me a job. Olga got me the chance to work for a real company and start my business career. With a new job working with her, I started thinking about asking Kim to marry me. We got engaged in September 1980 and married in November of 1981. We were both 23 years old.

As plans for our wedding got underway, I always believed that George would be my best man. I never thought differently. I called George and told him that he would be my best man (I never asked – I just assumed), and I told him the date of the wedding. I should mention that George was divorced at the time, and his life was full of his own issues. To my tremendous disappointment, my brother told me that he would not be able to attend the wedding, and I needed to find a new best man. I'm not going to kid anyone. It was a blow to me that George wouldn't be there. This was my wedding! But, to be honest, while I was disappointed, it wasn't like I ever turned my back on my brother or stopped talking to him or loving him. Nothing like that ever happened. We didn't talk much at that time of our lives; we just moved on. It wasn't until I was much older that we talked about how much I wanted him at the wedding. And, to my brother's credit, when we talked about it, he did acknowledge that he should have been there and that he was truly sorry that he didn't make it a priority. That was enough for me.

Kim and I were married at St. Francis Catholic Church on November 14, 1981, in a heartwarming ceremony. A great reception followed, with Kim and I off the next morning for a Caribbean Cruise. Those wonderful moments in your life go by in a blink of an eye.

The most devastating event of our young marriage happened in early September of 1984. Kim wasn't feeling well and stayed home from work on a Thursday. She wasn't feeling any better on Friday but wanted to go to work. Her company had a company picnic on Saturday, and she wanted to go. She got ready for work on Friday morning (I had already left the house for work myself), and on her way to the office, she passed out completely while driving and was involved in a horrible automobile accident. She was rushed to the hospital in critical condition. She managed to give the care workers my phone number, and they called me. I, along with my brother-in-law, Jim, rushed to the hospital. When I got there, Kim was awake but hurting bad. She suffered head injuries, and at the moment, no one knew how bad. She had many cuts from hitting her head on the windshield and side passenger window. She was in the emergency room, and they did many tests. She had a few deep cuts, but the most serious injury was a broken jaw - it was broken in three places. She had a lot of swelling, and the doctor decided to wait 2 days before he would do surgery to repair her broken jaw. She was in the hospital for 5 days and came home with her jaw wired shut as well as numerous stitches. We thought that after several months, Kim had recovered fully from the accident; we were wrong.

Kim suffered blood clots in her brain as a result of the accident. In her case, the clots did not cause any trouble for a couple of years. Ultimately, Kim developed the weird sensation of hearing her heartbeat in her ear. Several tests had not uncovered any issues. We never gave any thought to any issue related to the years earlier accident. It wasn't until 1988, when Kim finally went to Loyola University Medical school, that a doctor finally uncovered that she was suffering from hydrocephalus, a condition of fluid buildup in the brain. Her surgery to correct the hydrocephalus was successful, and the issue improved. When Kim gave birth to our third son, Eric, in 1991, she suffered a failure of the tube that was draining fluid from her brain. She needed to have emergency surgery to relieve the pressure on her brain. She was transferred back to Loyola, where the same doctor performed another surgery on her. It was a very difficult time; Kim was in bad shape. We had two young children at the house, and our newest son was still in the baby unit at the hospital. With God's strength, we were able to get Kim back healthy, and within two weeks, life seemed to settle. But, as with many challenges, this one just didn't go away. 6 weeks later, Kim suffered another failure of the tube that drained fluid from her brain. We rushed her back to the hospital, where another surgery was scheduled. This time, the doctors relocated the valve that allowed the fluid to drain from her head to her stomach. That seemed to work, and we have been blessed that she has not suffered any other issues with her hydrocephalus.

As mentioned, Kim and I had three wonderful sons: Andrew, Matthew, and Eric. I say wonderful, but believe me, children carry many challenges. And our sons certainly provided many. But, still, we wouldn't change our decision to have children. Ever.

About 10 years into our marriage, George called. He had a long story to tell me, and what a story it was. Again, I think I was misled when I was younger. I didn't know that George was given an ultimatum to enlist in the military, and I certainly did not know that a young George had gotten an equally young neighborhood girl named Barbara pregnant. I guess George's trouble with the law and Barbara's pregnancy happened about the same time. Barbara had made the very difficult decision (but I believe the correct one) to give the baby to Catholic charities and offer her for adoption. George had told me this story, and I had a tough time understanding this because, for almost 25 years, I had never known. Then, George told me the most important part of the story: he was making the commitment to find his daughter, that was given to adoption long ago. If you know my brother, when he is focused on something, it gets his full attention. And more often than not, he is successful in achieving his planned outcome. Well, this time was no different. After several frustrating discussions with Catholic charities and several months of leads and dead-ends, George was able to find his long-lost daughter, Karen. When he spoke with her for the first time, a 3-hour-long conversation uncovered that Karen and her husband lived 30 minutes from us. George asked me to call her, which I did almost immediately. However, Karen didn't answer the phone. I repeatedly called throughout the day, but I didn't connect with her. The next morning, which was a Sunday, Karen called our house very early. She said that after her call with George, she went over to her adoptive parents (the Wilcox's) house, and they talked about George's call for the rest of the day. She asked if she could come over to our house. She was at our door within the hour. Opening the door, Karen easily looked like George's daughter. There was no mistake; we could pick her out of the crowd. She was part of the family.

A bit after learning about Karen, I received another call from George. This was another call that rocked me. A lot of things happened to George when he was young, but one of them was not finishing high school. After the military, George settled in southern California and began a very strong entrepreneurial career. Even without a formal education, George was street smart, and he had a tremendous work ethic. He always worked hard. George was able to start his own company and, for a very long time, built a very successful specialty machining company, employing as many as thirty people. Employees included George's daughter and son, Lynne, and Lenny. I should also mention that George employed our youngest son, Eric, for over a year (more on that later).

While building his company, George had many customers, and I'm sure he took his fair share of risks. Entrepreneurs take risks; it's part of who they are. George's company, Omni Machine, had several important customers, and one of them was the U.S. government. During the process of manufacturing some parts for the government, George falsified records associated with the manufacturing of those parts, and the government was unforgiving. George was charged with Mail Fraud and received a felony sentence of 6 months in prison. Visiting him at a Federal Penitentiary in Las Vegas was not a particularly good day. George's inner strength got him through that period, and once released, he focused back on building his company.

At the end of 1992, I was working for AT&T. To my surprise, they offered me a relocation to Dallas, TX. I never thought we would ever live anyplace other than Chicago. Kim was thrilled to get out of Chicago and out of the cold weather. We moved to Southlake, TX, in March of 1993. Kim made a move super easy for me. She took care of everything, including our three boys. Southlake was a wonderful place to live and equally as wonderful of a place to raise a young family.

Our son, Andrew, seemed to sail through most of his childhood experiences with happiness and success. Our middle son, Matthew, on the other hand, always challenged Kim and I. He didn't have a question for us. He had 50 questions for us. He was always feeling shortchanged, regardless of the issue or situation. Eric, our youngest son, had the most emotional and personal feelings. I was so naïve with Eric. I believed whatever the situation, Eric would grow out of it. I should have been as smart as Kim and should have realized that Eric wasn't growing out of things, he was getting deeper into some very bad issues.

Not being able to control a young teenager led us to enroll Eric in a boarding school. Calling it a "boarding school" is being kind. Eric was in a lockdown facility, and they tried to reprogram his way of thinking. Again, I was naïve. Eric was simply going through the motions and couldn't wait to get out and get back to the life of non-conformity. Drugs became a part of his day-to-day life. Everything we tried did not result in much improvement. Enter into this picture – George.

George felt that Kim and I were being far too controlling as parents and that Eric was just a kid. George offered to give Eric the first big break in his young life. Eric could go out to southern California for the summer, where he could work for George, and he could also live with George and Anna.

Eric might have started his California chapter on the right side with George, but it didn't take long for his addiction to control his many poor judgements. In the end, Eric moved back to Dallas, and George admitted that Kim and I did all we could. And, even though George thought he was helping, he realized that Eric was out of control. I'll spare all of us the details of the interim years, but Eric finally had a reckoning with himself and sought help from Kim. She never gave up on him. Kim got Eric to a treatment facility in Utah, and Eric has turned every aspect of his life around and is now on the very best path that God has provided for him.

The boys grew up. Andrew was the first to formally move out of the house. But, it could be argued that it was Matthew that made a move first. Andrew graduated from college, and he came home for a bit before getting his own apartment. Matthew was in a rented house in Wichita Falls, TX, while he was attending Midwestern State University. When Matthew gave up on school, he moved back to Dallas. But he moved straight into mom's house in Denton. Mom was having a hard time living on her own, so Frieda had mom move in with her. She lived just down the street from mom.

Allow me to back up a bit - Mom and Dad were living in Wisconsin. We had asked them to make a move to Texas many times without success. Cathy, Frieda's daughter, was the one that finally had the conversation with Mom and Dad to convince them to move. It was wonderful. They moved into the Denton house in September of 2006. It was great to have them living only 30 minutes away. At the end of their first year in Texas, Dad had surgery to fix a back problem that he had had for a long time. Surgery was very hard on him, and it took a full six months for him to recover. Then, shortly after recovering from back surgery, he was diagnosed with cancer. He went into the hospital for some tests in mid-January 2008. He died 18 days later, on February 8, 2008; he was 80 years old. It was a sad day. Mom stayed strong and lived on her own for the next 7 years. During her last year with us, she moved in with Frieda. Mom died of natural causes on September 18, 2016, at 91 years old. Frieda was a wonderful caregiver. She selflessly took care of both Mom and Dad during their medical challenges. It was almost a full-time job. She did something that I admit I couldn't do. I give her all the credit for being the one who gave up so much for the benefit of Mom and Dad. During her last years, Mom wasn't the most patient woman. Freida handled it all without complaint.

Kim and I sold the big house in Southlake during the summer of 2013. Eighteen months earlier, we bought a second house in Naples, FL. I have always been a bit of a difficult type of a husband. I worked hard to convince Kim that we needed a second home. At the time, we were too young to consider retirement, so I looked at it as an investment property. We thought about getting a house in southern California near George. We looked, but we really couldn't afford much there. We had friends that moved from Texas to the west coast of Florida, so we looked there. Olga's daughter, Rebecca, was getting married, and the wedding was in the Florida Keys. We went out to the wedding a couple of days early to look at houses. We didn't find a house during that trip, but it at least made the decision to move to Florida more of a possibility. Kim started looking at houses online, and I started looking a bit as well. We found one house that stood out in Naples, FL. The house was just out of foreclosure, and the bank wanted to sell it quickly. We made an offer and then another offer before the bank accepted. In December 2011, we became the owners of our new home in Naples, FL.

I was still working, so we wanted a new Texas house that would be easy to maintain and could make it easy for us to leave and go to the Florida house for weeks at a time. We bought a house in Coppell, TX. It was a villa-type home with no outside maintenance, and it was easy to lock up and go to Florida. Over the years, Kim fell in love with the Florida house. She completely redid everything, and she made it our home. We sold the Texas house in December 2019, just before the worldwide pandemic, Covid-19, hit. Kim was already at the Florida house when I made the final move. It was great to own one house and not have to deal with two of everything. We love living in Florida, which was something I didn't think I would ever say. Olga and Jim always knew their futures were in Florida, but we didn't. But, we both will admit that this is really nice.

I retired to a life of the relaxed and casual; that was in April of 2021. I was really looking forward to retirement, but then I accepted a new full-time job in January 2022. A new chapter begins. Kim, the boys, and Ashley are all doing well. God is on our side and watching over us. We are blessed. Today is a good day.

"If you are on the path that God has chosen for you – you need never ask where it leads".

From Karen

I grew up knowing that I was adopted, along with my younger brother and sister. My adopted parents were always supportive of the idea of my someday searching for my biological parents, but I assured them that this was not something I was interested in pursuing. I never wanted them to feel that I was dissatisfied with the life they had given me, and I likely would never have searched for either of my birth parents as a result. However, I was always curious about them.... Did I resemble either of them in any way? What was my true ethnicity? What were their lives like now? When I was in my early 20s, I was taking a graduate class in group counseling. We were all required to attend a support group meeting that applied to us in some way. I chose to attend a local session of a group called Adoption Triangle. It was formed to assist adoptees in finding their biological parents and vice versa and to provide support during this process from other members. Just like everyone attending for the first time, I filled out a card with the sparse information I knew about my adoption: my mother's first name, the hospital where I was born, and the name of the agency through which I was adopted. Little did I know that just a few years later, the card I had filled out would change my life. In October of 1990, when I was 25, and after just having gotten married a few months earlier, I received a phone call from the leader of the Adoption Triangle, stating that my birth father was trying to locate me! I was in shock but quickly gave her permission to pass on my name and phone number to him. He called me almost immediately, explaining that he was advised by a private detective to contact an adoption search agency to try and locate me. Of all the agencies out there, he'd chosen the one I'd walked into a few years earlier as part of my graduate studies. The card I'd filled outmatched the information he had, and the rest is history. After he reached out to me, he gave me the most wonderful news: he had three other daughters and a son, and I couldn't wait to meet them! Additionally, George was married to Ana, the mother of my two younger sisters. I loved her from the moment I met her, and I still adore her and feel so lucky to have her in my life. From the moment I met my three beautiful sisters, Lynne, Alex, and Niki, and my brother, Lenny, I felt blessed, and I will always be so grateful to my dad for giving my husband, my children, and myself this amazing family. My daughter, Monica, and son, Trevor, grew up knowing all of the Lisenkos as their family. Unfortunately, we lost our beloved son Trevor in 2020, who was serving as a Marine in Bahrain at the time. He adored this family and admired his grandpa so much. In addition to the amazing siblings, aunts, uncles, and grandparents my father's search has provided me with, he was also able to track down my birth mother and her daughter, who was living in the same general area as we were in at the time. As a result, my children have grown up with even more family members surrounding them. I am so grateful for the way my father, George Lisenko, and his entire family have embraced all of us. Thanks, Dad.

From Lynne

My name is Lynne Durousseau. and I am George's second eldest daughter. I was born on June 19, 1968. My mom is Lelah Cox, and she was my dad's first wife. She is also the mother of my younger brother, Lenny Lisenko.

After my parent's split up (eventually divorcing), I lived with my dad for a few years when I was 14 years old. Then, eventually went back to living with my mom. I had some great times living with my dad. I still miss him making us pork chops and fried potatoes with salsa. I, of course, have tried to make them myself, but they were never quite as good as dads. I remember how he was always the funny guy, and my girlfriends thought he was so handsome, which he was. But, being 14, I was always so embarrassed, ha-ha. I remember the day he taught me to drive, and he taught me in his T-top Trans-Am. How awesome, right? All of my school friends thought it was the coolest car.

After I graduated high school, Dad offered me a job at his company, Omni Machine. I went to work for him in 1986. I left Omni to try management in the restaurant business when I was 25. After about 2 years, I returned to Omni and worked for Dad until February 2020. My now husband, Chris, also worked for Omni for almost 15 years until 2015. Although working with family was sometimes challenging, I still enjoyed working with my dad and my brother. I'm grateful for all the good times we had, and I miss seeing them 5 days a week.

I now live in Lake Havasu City, AZ, with my husband, Chris, and my fur babies, Dusty and Dena. I miss seeing all the family, but I'm so grateful to have been given the opportunity to move here. We absolutely love living here.

I'm so glad my dad decided to write a book about his life. I, as well as many others, always thought he should. He has been through so much and has accomplished so much. He/We have such a beautiful family. I'm lucky to have wonderful parents, including both my step-parents, whom I love very much. I know he is proud of all of us kids, and we are proud of him.

I love you, Dad. I can't wait to read your book.

With love, your daughter,

Lynne Durousseau

From Ana

This is Ana, George's wife! As you may know, I was born and raised in a district named Miraflores in Lima, Peru. I came to the USA to visit different states and fell in love with California! Since I arrived in 1981, I have lived in the city of Anaheim (the home of Ana in German)!

George and I met at Bobby McGees, a discotheque in Long Beach mid-1982, and since then, we have been inseparable! George took me to Chicago to meet his mom, Galina, stepdad, Victor, and the rest of his siblings, who were all in Illinois at that time! It was love at first sight! I fell in love with them all immediately! They were and are the warmest and most welcoming family I have ever met. George and I got married on 5/12/84 in Las Vegas, NV.

Since I met George, I told him that I wanted to continue traveling like I've been doing since I was 16, and I also wanted to have kids... at least two because I was the only child of my parents!

In 1986, George and I welcomed our first baby, Alexandra, making Lynne, Lenny, and Karen, the older siblings. Lynne was 18 years old, and Lenny was 10 years old at that time! Then, in 1989, our second baby was born. With Alex, I knew all along that I was expecting a girl ... which was awesome. With the second one, we didn't know..., so we picked the name of Nicholas, but our baby turned out to be a girl – and Nicole became her name!

We both worked long hours and are very grateful to my mother, Irma, who babysat for us. We were lucky enough to have their grandma with us, and we hired a babysitter here and there, which allowed us to travel all the time! The first trip with George was, of course, Peru! Now, he knows how cosmopolitan Lima can be a rich country that offers beautiful coasts.... the beaches are awesome, the mountains with their magic and spectacular heights and Inca ruins, and the jungle was the delight of Alex and Niki. I think we have implanted the traveling bug in our kids! George and I always have and will continue traveling for as long as we can.

We have amazing daughters that now are amazing mothers themselves! Life gives you ups, downs, sadness, and happiness, and here we are 38 years later, enjoying the best times of our lives and are proud to be called "grandparents" to our adorable grandkids: Monika, Lauren, Hailey, Karley, and Mason!

PS: For sure, I consider myself the one who has helped George start his business and create Omni Machine Corp. Sadly, I was not able to work with him because we needed a second income to take care of our family as well as insurance coverage. And I'm glad, too, that I take care of the bills because having a 'collector' at home can create major expenses. I call myself the 'money lady'.

From Lenny

My name is Lenny, and I am 47 years old and the only son of my dad's 5 children. My wife, Denise, and I married 9 years ago. We share a wonderful daughter, Lauren, who is now 7 years old. I am also blessed with 2 bonus kids: Dylan, who is 20 years old, and Danica, who is 16 years old.

My parents have been divorced for as long as I can remember. Although I did not live with my dad when growing up, he was always in my life. He would come to get me on the weekends and on holidays as far back as I could remember. At sixteen, I started working with him at Omni, and that is when we started to become very close.

I stand at 6'5", and my dad stands at 6'4", so it is easy to tell that we are father and son. People tell me all the time how much I look like my dad. My wife and sister both tell me that we have the same mannerisms and posture. In fact, when I was around 14 years old, I saw a photo of my dad at the same age and thought it was surreal since we looked identical to each other. I developed some of the same interests as my dad, but other than those and our looks, our family would agree that our personalities are like night and day.

He's what everyone would call a 'straight-shooter'. He always said what was on his mind and heart, regardless of who or where we were. I appreciate this a lot about my dad because I never have to question his thoughts on anything since he is always very direct. He speaks to everyone in the same way, whether it is a family member, an employee, or a client. This directness takes some getting used to, but I believe it is what makes him endearing to everyone that knows him well.

My dad is also very strong-willed and passionate, whether it's work, hobbies, or his relationships. In his own words, he never believed in doing anything 'half-ass'. He is very dedicated to working and almost never has a sick day. The next day after coming home from the hospital, you will see him show up at work ready to go. He works hard and plays hard. He is known for his passion for traveling and collecting. He has traveled to more places than anybody I know and has collected vodka bottles, license plates, guns, and coins while he was at it. He loves to entertain and share his newest additions to his collections with guests.

As passionate as my dad is about work and his interests, I admire his generosity and loyalty to his family and friends the most. My dad was always strict at work, but his employees have stayed loyal over the years because he has always been willing to offer help whenever they needed it. He always gave more than what was asked and taught me to never ask anybody that borrows money what it's for. I remember that my dad was always loyal and willing to back me up when I needed him. This means a lot to me and made me feel like I could always trust him, no matter what.

Working together for nearly 30 years, next to my stepmom, I've probably spent the most time with him. We had lunch together every day and talked about anything and everything. Being his only son, I have always considered our relationship a little different than my sister's relationship with him (in a man-to-man sort of way). I have learned everything I know about the business and a lot about life and relationships from watching him. His passion for work and life showed me what determination and a strong work ethic could reward you. Most of all, his loyalty to his family is what I hope to keep showing my wife and children, as well.

Together with my wife, we continue to run the business my father built over 35 years ago. I am grateful for the opportunity to have spent all those years together with him and my sister, Lynne. I believe the time with them both has contributed to the person I am today.

I want to take this opportunity to tell my sister, Lynne, how great of a sister she is. She has done so much for me for most of my life. I don't know how to say 'thank you' enough. I couldn't have asked for a better big sister. You're the best, Lynne. I love you.

Dad, thank you for everything. I love you and consider myself lucky to have you not only as my dad but as my mentor and best friend.

From Alexandra

My name is Alexandra Hanna, and I was born on May 15, 1986. My Mom is Ana Lisenko, who is my dad's second wife. They had my younger sister, Nicole (Niki), and I. I currently live in Albuquerque, NM, where I met and married my husband, Jonathan Hanna. We got married on October 19, 2019. He has a son named Jonathan Hanna Jr., age 13. I got a couple of years of practice being a stepmom to him before we had our baby boy, Mason Hanna, born November 10, 2021. We also have our two Boxers, Daisy and Duke.

My Dad is unlike any other person I've ever met. He is unapologetic, opinionated, and harsh at times, but through all of that, he has a big heart. My Mom always said he would talk to the president the same way he would talk to the trash man. We are so different in many ways, so we butted heads quite often while I was in my teens. I'm always so worried about what everyone else thinks while he doesn't even think twice. I realize, though, that this is part of what has made him so successful.

Growing up, I remember him leaving before the sun came up and always working on Saturdays. The metal shavings from his machine shop were a permanent part of his Moccasins…he always wore those brown Moccasins. He is the definition of "hard work pays off." My Mom and Dad built a great life together. The other side to the serious hard worker is a disco dancing, oldies-loving collector of things. We always had the coolest house in the neighborhood because we had the soda machine, the mechanical horse, and the Jukebox. We listened to that Jukebox at every family event. I bugged my dad enough about not having one that he and my mom finally bought me a 1955 Seeburg and had it restored. They even drove it all the way out to New Mexico shortly after Mason was born. I'm excited for Mason to grow up with the oldies I listened to as a kid.

My Dad always means well and truly cares about people. We were out to dinner once at a place called Mustards, and he offered to buy a homeless Veteran a meal. Then he invited him to eat with us- it made for an interesting evening. The man was not all there but was certainly grateful. Caring about people is one of the things I'm happy to say I do have in common with him.

I remember several times growing up when I was so embarrassed. He would drive down Main St., Huntington Beach, in the Suburban with the windows rolled down, blasting the SOS band song 'Take your Time.' I also remember him and my mom dancing any chance they got. He had the most embarrassing dance moves. He says you "either got the moves or you don't." I hate to admit that I don't think I ever had them. I only came to appreciate all this later in life. Now I look back and laugh and am so grateful for those memories.

Over the years, I've heard many stories from my dad. Many of them, I wasn't told until after I was 16 years old because my mom would say we weren't old enough to hear them. She didn't want us getting any ideas. The stories we heard sounded like he was describing scenes from a movie. My dad lived life. He has seen and done things most will only ever see in a movie. We would always tell him- you should write a book - I'm glad he finally did.

From Niki

My name is Nicole, and I'm George's and Ana's baby, the youngest. I'm 33 years old and have been with my boyfriend, Michael, for 4 years. We have done so much in those past years, including purchasing 2 houses, starting a business, and traveling. Our biggest blessings have been our 2 daughters: Hailey, who is 20 months old, and Karley, who is 8 months old.

Growing up, I was a daddy's girl! I am like my dad in many ways: my love for disco and oldies, my artistic abilities, my loud and outgoing personality, my passion for helping the less fortunate, and my love for travel. I'm also very opinionated and hard-headed, just like him. My dad is one of a kind! Before I can introduce him to people, I warn them that he is very straightforward and has strong opinions. I always say, "You either love him, or you hate him." So far, everyone seems to love him!

I have always thought that he was the coolest dad alive. My girlfriend, Sasha, and I thought we were so cool getting picked up from Junior high in his lifted Excursion, with all the windows down and the song by the S.O.S Band, "Take Your Time," blasting. Until this day, it's one of my favorite songs!

When I was 16 years old, my parents bought me my first car: a 1966 Mustang painted in dynasty green. I still remember seeing it for the first time with a big red bow on it! I also burned copies of my dad's disco CDs. I had to have the good stuff!

We grew up with a jukebox in the garage, which was filled with the '50s, '60s, and 70's music! When I bought my first condo, my parents surprised me with the most amazing housewarming gift: a 1961 Princess Rock-ola! It was filled with the best songs! My dad has always been a dancer. He has the best dance moves! I have always loved dancing with my dad! Although it was embarrassing watching my parents dance back then, I love watching them now. Until this day, if a disco song comes on at a wedding or a party, my parents are the first ones out on the dance floor, getting down, literally.

Every one of my friends, including classmates, loved my dad. Since he is a Vietnam veteran, he was asked to speak in my 8th-grade history class. I had to warn my teacher that he would probably curse and not hold anything back. I was right! He brought in pictures and also his canteen that had been shot. To my surprise, she loved him so much that she asked him to stay for her following classes! People were coming up to me for weeks telling me that they loved my dad and that he was the coolest. I always thought my dad would have made a great history teacher! He knows more than most people about history and politics!

My dad has always been very generous. That is why I preferred to ask him for money over my mom. He always had the crisp stash of $100 dollar bills in his wallet! He's always been one to help those in need. I always say that my dad has the biggest heart and would give anyone the shirt off his own back if they needed one. I have countless memories of him giving the homeless money and food. My dad would pick up tabs for random people at restaurants all the time. I remember going to Denny's with my parents and seeing a group of my sister's friends at the table across the way and him just picking up the tab, just because. My sister's friends would come over and just hang out with my dad even when she wasn't home! They would smoke cigarettes together while he would tell them stories of his younger, wilder days.

We all grew up hearing his stories of his time in Germany and his teen years in Chicago. It was a rule that my dad couldn't tell us anything bad until we were 16! I'm excited to read this book and read the stories that I never got to hear.

Dad, I love you so much, and I'm so thankful God chose me to be your daughter! I'm happy you decided to write your book, although my kids will probably have to wait until they are 16 years old to read it!

In closing notes:

- I have always loved BEAUTIFUL women and believe my 5 kids come from beautiful women. And remember: the looks come from your choice of women

- Hard work and being persistent in the goals you set are the key to success.

- Live your life the way you see it and not the way other people see it.

- Hang out with good company and get rid of the bad ones

- You only have one life to live, so you must live it to your fullest.

- Treat people with respect and dignity and accept the same in return and if not "dump them"

- There is a big world out there, so try and see as much as you can of it.

- Always be a giver and not a taker. It will come back to you 10-fold.

- Always remember money is the root of all evil.

- Always be as honest as you can be, but when it comes to the IRS (Internal Revenue Service), be as dishonest as you can be.

- At this point in my life, I'm trying to live the good life, and all the credit goes to my wife, ANA. Without her, we would not have all the things and properties we have today. I truly believe I'd be lost without her.

Special thanks to Jessica Mosier and Mark Masters for all their help organizing the manuscript of my book.

CPSIA information can be obtained
at www.ICGtesting.com
Printed in the USA
LVHW060200121122
732945LV00044B/3170